Beginners' Guide
to
Herb Gardening

Beginners' Guide to
HERB
GARDENING

~ Yvonne Cuthbertson ~

GUILD OF MASTER CRAFTSMAN
PUBLICATIONS LTD

For my husband, Bob

First published 2001 by
Guild of Master Craftsman Publications Ltd
166 High Street, Lewes, East Sussex BN7 1XU

Text © Yvonne Cuthbertson 2001
© in the Work GMC Publications Ltd

Reprinted 2002

Illustrations by Penny Brown
Photographs on pages 20, 110, 112, 121, 126 © Harry Smith Collection
All other photographs © Yvonne Cuthbertson

ISBN 1 86108 198 7

British Cataloguing in Publication Data
A catalogue record of this book is available from the British Library

Cover design by Stonecastle Graphics

Book designed and edited by Margot Richardson

Colour separation by Viscan Graphics Pte Ltd (Singapore)
Printed by and bound by Kyodo (Singapore) under
the supervision of MRM Graphics, Winslow, Buckinghamshire, UK

CONTENTS

INTRODUCTION

Herb gardening is rather like embarking on a journey into the past; a nostalgic trip evocative of all the charm and delights of a more leisurely age. And probably the greatest joy of herb gardening is that it is easy, inexpensive and very satisfying as well as combining all the pleasures of the flower garden with the usefulness of the vegetable plot. A small amount of effort is soon rewarded by a treasury of shape, colour, texture and taste. Herbs are accommodating plants to grow and, given the right conditions, they will quickly reward you with vigorous, healthy growth, luxuriant foliage and rich, aromatic perfumes. They are now generally accepted as valuable garden plants in their own right, and can make stunning displays as well as being functional.

Herbs have held their place in our gardens for centuries and have a long association with the church: the monastery gardens are legendary. Herbs are attractive, romantic and

Feverfew produces masses of daisy-like flowers

Golden rod has upright stems and pointed leaves, and its yellow flowers are borne in late summer

Their aesthetic appeal and decorative and ornamental qualities are as important today as they have always been, with each plant having its own characteristic scent, foliage, texture and shape.

Herb gardens are pleasant places in which to walk, especially on a hot summer's day when their aromatic scents permeate the whole garden. There is also something very satisfying about stepping outside your

Cowslips are one of the best herbs for attracting bees during spring

timeless, reminiscent of bygone days when our ancestors cultivated them not only for their usefulness, but also for the 'magic' that surrounded them. Herb gardens also have a certain domestic quality, providing unity to the planting by giving it shape and purpose.

Nasturtiums make an excellent garnish for salads, giving them both colour and flavour

kitchen door and picking a handful of fragrant herbs. Herb gardens allow plenty of scope for the imagination, and herbs adapt to a number of styles and designs. Planning and planting them is fun. It prompts you to look at gardening books and catalogues, to visit nurseries, garden centres, existing herb gardens and even museums and libraries to do a bit of research as you collect your ideas and choose which herbs to grow. A decorative herb garden gives pleasure during every season if year-round interest is taken into account when planning it.

Everyone can grow herbs, even if they live in a flat or apartment. Many gardeners cultivate herbs in containers, which is an excellent idea if space is limited. The wide range and variety of herbs on offer nowadays make it easy to introduce them into any garden, whatever its size or design.

With today's ever-increasing interest in ecology, natural products and alternative medicines, herbs have once more come into their own. In addition to being utilitarian and practical, they are easy to introduce into any garden layout, thus allowing the gardener to find plants suitable for every situation. Herbs are ideal to make a garden that is unique and individual, and that always reflects the personal tastes of its creator.

1 DESIGNING AND PLANNING A HERB GARDEN

Herbs are a striking and invaluable feature of any garden, and a surprisingly large selection can be grown in a small amount of space, added to which, herbs are extremely adaptable and easy to cultivate. They can be planted in a variety of situations: the vegetable plot, the rockery and the herbaceous border, to name but a few. And yet, there is something extremely satisfying about having a separate, attractively designed herb garden: the impact of combined scents, shapes, textures and colours can be quite stunning.

SIZE

A herb garden can range from the smallest practical measurement, 1.8m (6ft) by 1.2m (4ft), to 3m (9ft 9in) square, to 7.6m (25ft) by 5.5m (18ft) or larger. This depends upon the space available, your chosen design, the herbs you wish to grow, and the time you have available for maintenance (although herbs are relatively maintenance free). However, don't be over-ambitious: start small, growing the herbs you will use initially and then adding to them later on.

A traditional American herb garden at the American Museum in Bath, England

LOCATION

Before you can actually plan the design of your herb garden, you need to establish where it is going to be located. Many herbs originated in Mediterranean countries and prefer plenty of sun, some exceptions being the mints (mentha), chervil (*Anthriscus cerefolium*), bergamot (*Monarda didyma*) and angelica (*Angelica archangelica*). The ideal position for your herb garden, therefore, is in a south- and/or west-facing part of the garden that slopes slightly towards the sun.

Always plant your herbs in the conditions they prefer. Make sure that you have easy access to them: firm, all-weather paths are essential. Remember also that some herbs are very choosy about soil and position, while others are extremely adaptable. For instance, rosemary (*Rosmarinus officinalis*) will grow almost anywhere, although it will not flourish in cold winters.

Most herbs, including hyssop, need sun to thrive

Honeysuckle can be trained around pillars

SHELTER

Herbs dislike wind, so a sheltered spot is important. This can be achieved simply and effectively by planting hedges of herbs such as English lavender (*Lavandula angustifolia*), rosemary, hyssop (*Hyssopus officinalis*), or traditional box (*Buxus sempervirens*), all of which will tolerate clipping. Alternatively, trellises with roses or honeysuckle trained up them will help. If you are able to site your garden within a walled area or behind a fence, so much the better. The garden could be 'walled in' with banks of earth which can afterwards be planted with pennyroyal (*Mentha pulegium*) or Roman chamomile (*Chamaemelum nobile*).

SOIL

The condition and quality of the soil is important to every herb garden design. Soil that is sodden after prolonged rain will need to have its water-draining ability improved, although most herbs will thrive on relatively poor soil, provided that it is not waterlogged. Often, improvement can be achieved quite easily by forking in coarse sand at the rate of 1.7–2.1 kg per sq m (4 lb per sq yd).

If, however, the drainage problem is more severe, this can be solved by the construction of a soakaway.

Constructing a soakaway

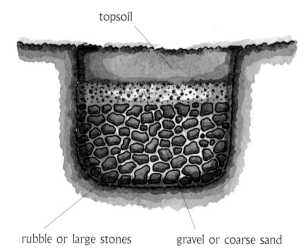

topsoil

rubble or large stones   gravel or coarse sand

STAGE 1: Dig a hole at least 60cm (2ft) square and 90cm (3ft) deep at the lowest point in the garden.

STAGE 2: Fill it to within 30cm (12in) of the top with rubble or large stones.

STAGE 3: Cover with a 15cm (6in) layer of gravel or coarse sand.

STAGE 4: Finish with a 15cm (6in) layer of topsoil to ground level.

Types of soil

The acidity or alkalinity of soil depends upon how much calcium it contains: too little and the soil is acid, too much and it is alkaline. These levels of calcium are measured by what is known as the pH scale which reads from 0–14. Soils with a pH above 7 are alkaline, those with a pH below 7 are acid. The pH of most soils lies somewhere between pH6 and pH 7.5 making them more or less neutral, and most herbs will tolerate these kinds of conditions. A pH reading of 7 is ideal.

You can determine the pH level of your own soil by buying a pH-testing kit from your local garden centre and following its simple instructions. The kit will indicate the approximate pH value. This approximation is usually good enough because all plants possess some tolerance.

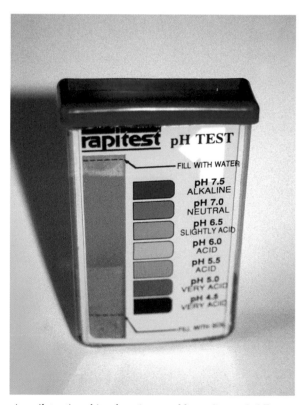

A soil-testing kit, showing a pH reading of 6.5, which denotes a slightly acid soil

Acid soil

Not many plants thrive in acid soil. The pH of slightly acid soil can be raised by the addition of lime. The best limes to use are ground chalk or limestone, the finer the grade the better, and they can be dug into your plot during preparation time.

Great care should always be taken when using lime because it is a caustic substance. Be sure to choose a day when no wind is blowing, and always keep children and pets well away from the area. A mask can be worn, if desired. Always wear gloves when handling, and make sure that it doesn't come into contact with the skin or the eyes. If it does, wash off immediately with cold water. Should there be any cause for concern, seek medical advice immediately.

Heavy clay soil

Heavy clay soil should be dug over in autumn and left exposed to winter frosts. Add large quantities of organic matter during late winter/early spring; its fibrous nature will help open up the soil and, gradually, smaller and smaller crumbs will form from the large clods of earth. Leaf mould and bark are excellent soil conditioners. Bark is best left on the surface to rot, after which it can then be worked into the soil. Seaweed and spent hops also do the job, as does spent mushroom compost. Plenty of organic matter such as this will need to be worked in, and added regularly every year. You could also add grit or sand but, while the texture of the soil will be altered, little will be done to improve its actual structure.

On the plus side, though, clay is probably one of the richest soils as it has the ability to hold on to plant foods and to release them slowly, and there are herbs that will thrive in it, such as comfrey (*Symphytum officinale*),

Horseradish will thrive in a clay soil

elecampane (*Inula helenium*), horseradish (*Armoracia rusticana*), Jacob's ladder (*Polemonium caeruleum*) and tansy (*Tanacetum vulgare*). Generally, though, plants will struggle in heavy clay soils. The ground easily becomes compacted because there are very few air spaces between the particles. So if your soil is really very heavy, you should, perhaps, consider growing your herbs in raised beds (see pages 76–7).

Light soil

A light, free-draining soil is usually low in nutrients and doesn't hold moisture. Mediterranean herbs will thrive under such conditions, but others will not. Herbs such as mints will benefit from the addition of organic matter four to five weeks before planting which will supply nutrients and help to retain moisture. Don't do this any earlier as you will risk the chance of it being leached by the rain. Humus contains gel-like substances which bind soil particles together to form crumbs, and also aid the retention of moisture due to their sponge-like properties.

Most ground needs a thorough digging in order to prepare it for a herb garden

FERTILIZERS

Fertilizer may be added to the soil ten to twelve days before planting. A compound fertilizer will contain nitrogen to encourage leaf and stem growth, potash to aid flower and fruit formation, and phosphate which will give a boost to roots. Try to avoid the use of artificial fertilizers. Organic or herbal fertilizers are best.

DIGGING YOUR PLOT

Before planting, you will need to dig your soil over thoroughly. Generally, soil only needs to be dug to one spade's depth. One exception is land surrounding a newly built house where builders have been using heavy machinery and have then placed a few centimetres of fresh soil over the compacted topsoil to make it look good. (This can also happen on ploughed farm land.) This will have left a hard layer of compacted earth below the surface soil which will impede drainage and prevent plants from rooting. In this case, double digging will be necessary.

Dig the plot over in autumn and, if single digging, throw the soil forwards as you go so that you have a neat trench alongside you. Put organic matter on the slope of the soil that has been thrown forwards, so that it will eventually become thoroughly mixed in through all levels of the soil. Refill the trenches with the amount of soil taken out to keep the digging level. In spring, turn the soil over thoroughly, removing all weeds and debris. Break it up with a spade or fork and then rake it until a fine tilth is obtained.

PLANTING

- Keep to recommended planting distances on the seed packets or, if the plants have been bought from a nursery or garden centre, to the planting distances shown on the labels.
- Harvest the herbs regularly. Trim them and keep them in check as necessary to control both their height and their spread and to keep your design or construction neat and well-defined.
- Remember that herbs will grow at different rates according to the soil in which they are planted, their position and the climate of the area in which you live. Some of them will also self-seed.
- The overall number of plants you use will depend upon the size of your design or construction.
- Note the season of interest of each herb.

PLANNING ON PAPER

Once you have decided on the size and site of your herb garden, it is important to plan it on paper so that you can be sure of blending the colours of foliage and flowers, and the textures of leaves, as well as avoiding planting tall herbs in front of mound-forming varieties.

Ask yourself what kind of design is suitable for your garden, what groups of plants you will grow, and if your garden will follow a theme or pattern. Draw to scale to make it easier to appreciate the size of the beds; to assess the proportions – height and spread – of the various herbs; and to compare the space between the beds with the dimensions of your plants. Measure carefully and make sure you position all your permanent features correctly. Don't forget to include nearby existing features such as hedges, fences, walls, large trees and the house itself.

A herb bed with traditional box hedging, clipped to give the bed its customary uniformity

A triangular edging of golden feverfew

Think where you are going to place your paths. A herb garden will need paths around its borders as well as between its beds. Ideally they should be wide enough for trundling a wheelbarrow along, and for wheelchair access, if applicable. If your garden is to be of an informal design, then the paths could be curved, but make sure that they lead somewhere: towards a seat, perhaps? And don't forget to place a focal point, which is traditional and which relieves the flatness: a bird bath, a sundial, or a potted bay tree are ideal. Ornaments, however, must never dominate or ruin the impact of your design. It is easy to destroy the elegance of your herb garden, so choose wisely.

Use separate sheets of paper for working out planting schemes. These can be altered, if necessary, when you have actually tried out possible variations in your garden. All-round interest should be considered. Herb gardens can look very bare in winter, so be sure to use some evergreen herbs such as rosemary, bay (*Laurus nobilis*), hyssop and rue (*Ruta*

graveolens) as the backbone of your design, planting them throughout according to their height. You should then think about the positioning of perennial herbs such as lemon balm (*Melissa officinalis*), fennel (*Foeniculum vulgare*), lovage (*Levisticum officinale*) and bergamot and, finally, annual herbs which should be arranged according to height, spread, colour of flowers and foliage, and texture of leaves.

Within your chosen design, herbs can be planted informally and arranged so that the culinary herbs are kept separate from pot-pourri ones, for example, or formally using just a few species of herbs in large numbers to create 'carpets' of herb bedding.

DESIGNS

Having chosen your site, you will need to think about the shape and size of your garden. In most gardens the shape is rectangular. But, whatever design you decide upon, remember that your herb garden must be practical.

A lot of herb gardens are informal and semi-formal, although the ones that have the greatest impact are usually formal. Remember that many herbs don't grow to their 'prescribed' sizes, while some of them romp away, often to twice their normal size. This can result in one plant masking another as it jostles for space and light so you will need to discover how various herbs will grow in your particular soil. It is also important to know the type of soil that you have and to note down the season of interest of each of your chosen plants: some will start to grow early in the year, others much later, and they will also flower at different times. Bear in mind foliage, colour and texture: you may wish to grade them or you might prefer to spread them randomly throughout.

FORMAL DESIGNS: KNOT GARDENS

Some formal, geometric herb gardens take the form of a knot, first recorded in the fifteenth century. Originally contained within a square- or rectangle-shaped plot, each knot pattern was precisely outlined by low, clipped hedges of evergreen herbs, such as box, cotton lavender (*Santolina chamaecyparissus*), hyssop and lavender. The designs themselves were often taken from family crests, heraldic devices, or the entwined initials of the garden's owners.

The keynote of such a garden was its traditional uniformity, a result of the types of hedging plants chosen and the way in which they were clipped.

Ideas from these traditional knot gardens can be adapted and included in today's smaller garden. Knot gardens also have the advantage of the herbs being within easy reach for harvesting and upkeep. Although precision is vital to this kind of design, so is frequent maintenance so that the low hedges remain trim and the whole geometrical symmetry neat.

A geometric herb garden in the form of a knot at The Red Lodge in Bristol, England

Planting suggestions

Hedges
Box (*Buxus sempervirens*)
Cotton lavender (*Santolina chamaecyparissus*)
Lavenders (lavandula)
Rosemary (*Rosmarinus officinalis*)
Shrubby germander (*Teucrium fruticans*)
Winter savory (*Satureja montana*)

Tall herbs
Angelica (*Angelica archangelica*)
Elecampane (*Inula helenium*)
Fennel (*Foeniculum vulgare*)
Lovage (*Levisticum officinale*)
Mullein (*Verbascum thapsus*)

Centrepieces
Sundial, bird bath, statue, potted bay tree

Paths
Bricks, pebbles, gravel

Medium-sized herbs
Coriander (*Coriandrum sativum*)
Feverfew (*Tanacetum parthenium* formerly
    Chrysanthemum)
Hyssop (*Hyssopus officinalis*)
Lemon balm (*Melissa officinalis*)
Mints (mentha)
Sages (salvia)
Sweet basil (*Ocimum basilicum*)
Tarragon (*Artemisia dracunculus*)

Short and edging herbs
Anise (*Pimpinella anisum*)
Basil thyme (*Acinos arvensis*)
Chives (*Allium schoenoprasum*)
Double chamomile (*Chamaemelum nobile* 'Flore Pleno')
Parsley (*Petroselinum crispum*)
Pennyroyal (*Mentha pulegium*)
Sweet marjoram (*Origanum majorana*)
Thymes (thymus)

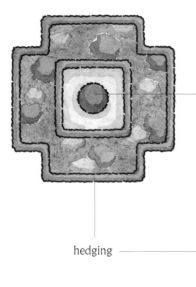

centrepiece / focal point

hedging

Examples of knot garden designs

Creating a knot garden

STAGE 1: Select your site and determine its measurements. Draw your proposed design to scale on graph paper. This will allow you to visualize the size of the beds, to assess the proper placement of plants and to obtain a good, overall image of your knot.

STAGE 2: Dig your soil, removing all perennial weeds and large stones. Dig in humus/rich organic matter as you go along.

STAGE 3: You are now ready to transfer the design to the plot. Working from your scaled paper plan, measure out the design on the ground. Mark it with the string and stakes/pegs, then fill in the details with the chalk powder. If you are making a square garden, double check that all sides of the plot are of equal length, and that the corners are all at right angles, using the piece of wood with a right-angle.

STAGE 4: Place the focal point – sundial, bird bath, or formal rose bush – in the centre.

STAGE 5: Plant the hedging herbs that will outline and define your knot at their planting

You will need:
Measuring tape
Humus/organic matter (see page 7)
Ball of string
Short wooden stakes or pegs
Squeezable bottle of chalk dust
Piece of wood with a right-angle
Selection of herbs

distances. Box (*Buxus sempervirens*), for example, always a great favourite, needs a planting distance of 20cm (8in). When the edging herbs begin to spread, clip their tops, and the sides that face the walks or beds, so that they are encouraged to grow more quickly.

STAGE 6: Once the hedging plants are in place, the beds can be planted with herbs, and the pathways laid.

STAGE 7: Plant the evergreen and perennial herbs first, remembering to give plenty of thought to their foliage and flower colour. When everything is planted, water in well and keep watered until the herbs are well established.

Hedging of box, lavender or rosemary, surrounding beds of other herbs, is an essential for knot gardens

FORMAL DESIGNS: CHESSBOARD

A chessboard design uses paving slabs, attractively laid in a square chessboard formation. The spaces between the paving slabs, which are exactly the same size as the slabs themselves, are left open to the soil and are used for planting the herbs.

Creating a chessboard garden

You will need:
Paving slabs, number depending on
   size of design
Ball of string
Short wooden stakes or pegs
Spirit level
Length of board
Piece of wood with a right-angle
Garden tools
Humus/organic matter (see page 7)
Selection of herbs

Planting suggestions

Plant one herb per square
Borage (*Borago officinalis*)
Chives (*Allium schoenoprasum*)
German chamomile (*Matricaria recutita*)
Golden marjoram (*Origanum vulgare* 'Aureum')
Lavenders (lavandula)
Pineapple mint (*Mentha suaveolens* 'Variegata')
Purple leaved sage (*Salvia officinalis* 'Purpurascens')
Thymes:
   Caraway thyme (*Thymus herba–barona*)
   Golden thyme (*Thymus citriodorus* 'Aureus')
   Thyme (*Thymus vulgaris* 'Silver Posie')
   Variegated thyme (*Thymus* x *citrodorus* 'Silver Queen')

A finished chessboard garden

STAGE 1: Select your site and determine its measurements, taking into account the number and size of the paving slabs you intend to use. Remember to allow for possible breakages when buying the slabs.

STAGE 2: Draw your plan to scale, marking in position of paving slabs, areas of soil, focal point and herb plantings.

STAGE 3: Using string and stakes/pegs, mark out the whole area of your plot.

STAGE 4: Dig the soil, removing all perennial weeds and large stones. Dig in humus/rich organic matter as you go along.

STAGE 5: Rake soil to a fine tilth and level with the edge of the board to ensure that the plot is quite flat.

STAGE 6: If you are making a square garden, check that all sides of the plot are of equal length, and that the corners are all at right angles, using the wood with a right-angle.

STAGE 7: Lay the first slab in the top left-hand corner, using the string as a guide. Make sure that it rests snugly against the string. Using a spirit level, check that the slab is level in all directions. If it isn't, add or remove a little soil underneath one corner.

STAGE 8: Miss out a space of earth equal to the slab width and then lay your next stone.

STAGE 9: Repeat this procedure along the length of the plot, again resting the final slab snugly against the string.

STAGE 10: Start the second row by placing the first slab in front of the first area of soil in the completed row with the corners touching, again using your spirit level. Complete the row of alternate slabs and soil.

STAGE 11: Lay the third row by again placing the first slab in front of the soil in the previous row and continue along, making sure that the first and last slabs lay snugly against the string.

STAGE 12: Continue in this way until the total area has been completed, leaving you with a chessboard-effect herb garden.

STAGE 13: Remove the string and stakes/pegs. You can, if you wish, lay a gravel path, add gravel around the edges, or plant a hedge around the chessboard using, for example, cotton lavender.

STAGE 14: You are now ready to plant the herbs. When planted, water in well and keep watered until the herbs are well established.

FORMAL DESIGNS: HERB CARTWHEEL

Another bold, formal design is a herb cartwheel – an all-time favourite. The wheel is treated with preservative, painted on one side with white exterior paint, and set lightly into the prepared soil. A variety of different herbs of similar heights and rates of growth are planted between the spokes. This creates a quickly made miniature herb garden. Alternatively, because old wooden cartwheels are both expensive and hard to come by, you could make your own replica from halved log rolls of manageable size.

Be aware of recommended planting distances and divide or transfer plants to another part of the garden if and when they outgrow the design, so that the cartwheel always looks neat and compact. Do not allow it to become overgrown, straggly, or untidy.

You will need:

Log rolls: the number will depend upon the size of the rolls and of your proposed wheel. Separate the logs from the wire that holds them when purchased, paint with preservative and varnish with an exterior varnish or paint.

Flower pot or bulb bowl for the hub of the wheel, varnished or painted.

Ball of string

Short wooden stakes or pegs

Wooden mallet

Selection of herbs

Example size

A diameter of 1.8m (6ft)

A herb wheel, about six weeks after planting

Planting suggestions

Chives (*Allium schoenoprasum*): Height 10–60cm (4–24in), spread 30cm (12in). Use three plants.

Compact marjoram (*Origanum vulgare* 'Compactum'): Height 15cm (6in), spread 30cm (12in). Use three plants.

Corsican mint (*Mentha requienii*): Height 2–10cm (1–4in), spread indefinite. Use one plant.

Dwarf lavender (*Lavandula angustifolia* 'Nana Alba'): Height 15–30cm (6–12in), spread 15–45cm (6–18in). Use two plants.

Golden lemon thyme (*Thymus* x *citriodorus* 'Aureus'): Height 10–15cm (6–12in), spread 60cm (24in). Use one plant.

Marjoram (*Origanum vulgare* 'White Anniversary'): Height 15–25cm (6–10in), spread 15–20cm (6–8in). Use four plants.

Nasturtium (*Tropaeolum majus* 'Alaska'): Height and spread 30cm (12in). Use three plants.

Parsley (*Petroselinum crispum*): Height 30–80cm (12–32in), sprea: 30cm (12in). Use three plants.

Pennyroyal (*Mentha pulegium*): Height 10–40cm (4–16in), spread indefinite. Use one plant.

Creating a log-roll cartwheel

STAGE 2: Dig the soil, removing turf or gravel (if necessary) and all perennial weeds and large stones. Dig in humus/rich organic matter as you go along. Remove some of the topsoil, placing the topsoil on a sheet of polythene. Loosen the subsoil.

STAGE 1: Mark out the area using two wooden stakes/pegs and a piece of string. Attach the string to one of the pegs and plunge it into the ground at the centre of the proposed circle. Attach the second peg to the end of the string, at the required radius of the circle. Holding the string taut, mark out the circumference of the circle on the ground.

STAGE 3: Place the bulb bowl or flower pot at the centre of the circle.

STAGE 4: Divide the circle into quarters by positioning the logs in the form of a cross. Tap into place.

STAGE 6: Position the edging logs and tap firmly with the mallet. Replace some of the excavated topsoil into each of these segments.

STAGE 5: Place two more lines of logs diagonally so that you have eight separate segments of equal size, and tap into position.

STAGE 7: Plant the herbs, remembering to allow for growth and spread. Water in well and keep watered until well established.

The herb wheel when fully planted

FORMAL DESIGNS: HERB LADDER

An old wooden ladder can be used for this design, but it should be treated with a preservative before use, and then stained or painted on one side with exterior paint. Place it in position in prepared soil and plant your herbs between the rungs of the ladder. Alternatively, bricks can be used to achieve the same effect. The outside uprights of the 'ladder' should be positioned first and the brick 'rungs' fitted in afterwards.

Example size

1.8m (6ft) long, giving six planting spaces of 38 x 30cm (15 x 12in).

Planting suggestions

Chives (*Allium schoenoprasum*):
    Height 10–60cm (4–24in), spread 30cm (12in). Use two plants.
Double chamomile (*Chamaemelum nobile* 'Flore Pleno'):
    Height 15cm (6in), spread 45cm (18in). Use one plant.
Lemon thyme (*Thymus* x *citriodorus*):
    Height 25–30cm (10–12in), spread 60cm (24in). Use one plant.
Parsley (*Petroselinum crispum*):
    Height 30–80cm (12–32in), spread 30cm (12 in). Use three plants.
Pennyroyal (*Mentha pulegium*):
    Height 10–40cm (4–16in), spread indefinite. Use one plant.
Sweet marjoram (*Origanum majorana*):
    Height 60cm (24in), spread 45cm (18in). Use one plant.

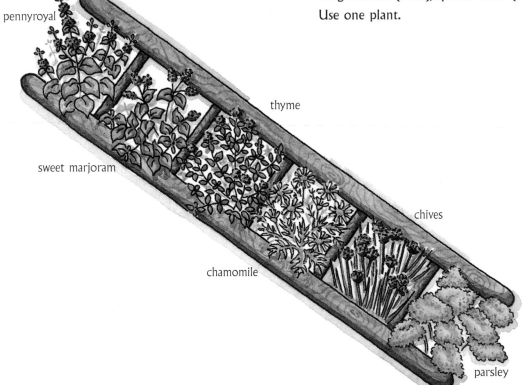

pennyroyal

sweet marjoram

thyme

chamomile

chives

parsley

Plan for herb ladder

SEMI-FORMAL DESIGNS: HERB BORDER

Planted in a well-drained, sunny position, a border of mixed herbs will provide interest and colour to the garden. Those noted for their attractive foliage should be included, for example tansy and the sages, along with those with wonderful aromatic foliage such as rosemary and lavender.

Herbs with taller habit should be planted towards the back – angelica, lovage and elecampane are a few examples – with the smaller plants to the front. The border can be edged with chives, parsley or thyme and backed by medium-sized herbs such as cotton lavender, marjoram, winter savory or sweet cicely (*Myrrhis odorata*). To avoid formal planting, the herbs should be set out in groups of three or five – uneven numbers are best – any gaps being filled with colourful annuals such as blue borage or red poppies.

Example size
9.25m (30ft) long by 2.3m (7ft 6in) wide.

A plan for a semi-formal herb border

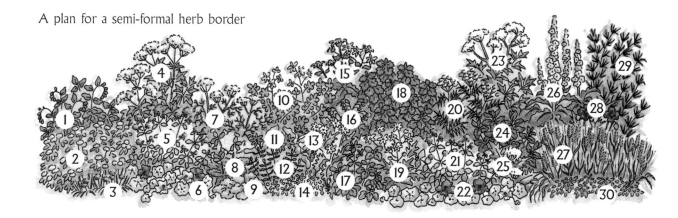

Lush growth in an informal corner herb bed

Key to illustration:

1	Comfrey	16	Borage
2	Cotton lavender	17	Sweet marjoram
3	Chives	18	Variegated lemon balm
4	Lovage	19	Feverfew
5	Golden marjoram	20	Tansy
6	Trailing nasturtium	21	Golden marjoram
7	Dill	22	Trailing nasturtiums
8	Cowslips	23	Angelica
9	Parsley	24	Sage
10	Rue	25	Sweet cicely
11	Pot marigolds	26	Mullein
12	Winter savory	27	Lavender
13	Chamomile	28	Poppies
14	Golden thyme	29	Rosemary
15	Elecampane	30	Thyme 'Silver Posie'

Planting suggestions

Tall herbs

Angelica (*Angelica archangelica*): Height 1–2.5m (3–8ft), spread 45cm–1.1m (18–43in). Use one plant.

Elecampane (*Inula helenium*): Height 3m (10ft), spread 1.5m (5ft). Use one plant.

Fennel (*Foeniculum vulgare*): Height 2m (6ft 6in), spread 45cm (18in). Use one plant.

Lovage (*Levisticum officinale*): Height 2m (6ft 6in), spread 1m (39in). Use one plant.

Mullein (*Verbascum thapsus*): Height 2m (6ft 6in), spread 1m (39in). Use two plants.

Rosemary (*Rosmarinus officinalis*): Height and spread 2m (6ft 6in). Use one plant.

Medium-sized herbs

Cotton lavender (*Santolina chamaecyparissus*): Height 20–50cm (8–20in), spread 60cm (24in). Use three.

Curry plant (*Helichrysum italicum* syn. *H angustifolium*): Height 60cm (24in), spread 1m (39in). Use one.

Feverfew (*Tanacetum parthenium* formerly *Chrysanthemum*): Height 60cm (24in), spread 45cm (18in). Use three.

Golden marjoram (*Origanum vulgare* 'Aureum'): Height and spread 75cm (30in). Use three plants.

Hyssop (*Hyssopus officinalis*): Height 45–60cm (18–24in), spread 60–90cm (24–36in). Use one plant.

Lemon balm (*Melissa officinalis*): Height 30–80cm (12–32in), spread 30–45cm (12–18in). Use five plants.

Mints (*mentha*): Height variable, spread indefinite. Use one plant.

Rue (*Ruta graveolens*): Height 60cm (24in), spread 45cm (18in). Use five plants.

Sages (*salvia*): Height and spread variable, depending on the species. Use three plants.

Sweet cicely (*Myrrhis odorata*): Height 1–2m (3–6ft 6in), spread 60cm–1.2m (2–4ft). Use one plant.

Tarragon (*Artemisia dracunculus*): Height 45cm–1m (18–39in), spread 30–38cm (12–15in). Use three.

Winter savory (*Satureja montana*): Height 10–40cm (4–16in), spread 7–20cm (3–8in). Use five plants.

Colourful annuals

Borage (*Borago officinalis*): Height 30cm–1m (12–39in), spread 15–30cm (6–12in). Use three plants.

Poppies (*papaver*): Height and spread variable, depending on the species. Use three plants.

Pot marigold (*Calendula officinalis*): Height and spread 50–70cm (20–28in). Use two plants.

Small plants

Cowslips (*Primula veris*): Height and spread 15–20cm (6–8in). Use five plants.

Heartsease or wild pansies (*Viola tricolor*): Height and spread 38cm (15in). Use three plants.

Primroses (*Primula vulgaris*): Height 15cm (6in), spread 25cm (10in). Use five plants.

Edging herbs

Chives (*Allium schoenoprasum*): Height 10–60cm (4–24in), spread 30cm (12in). Use two plants.

Double chamomile (*Chamaemelum nobile* 'Flore Pleno'): Height 15cm (6in), spread 45cm (18in). Use three.

Parsley (*Petroselinum crispum*): Height 30–80cm (12–32in), spread 30cm (12 in). Use two plants.

Thymes (*thymus*): Height and spread variable, depending on species. Use two plants.

Trailing nasturtium (*Tropaeolum majus* 'Trailing Mixed'): Height 4–6in (10–15cm), spread up to 2m (6ft 6in). Use three plants.

INFORMAL HERB GARDENS

Whether by accident or design, herb beds are usually informal because many herbs fail to know their proper limits. An informal garden can be beautiful as plants jostle for space and overflow on to pathways, but you will need to take care that your herbs don't get out of control. When planning an informal herb garden, follow your own intuition rather than a regular plan or pattern as informal gardens tend to obscure boundaries. Planting should be close so that no soil is visible once the plants are established. Herbs that self-seed – foxglove (*Digitalis purpurea*), evening primrose (*Oenothera biennis*) and borage, for example – will grow on in a random fashion. Remember to plant in informal groupings.

An informal, old-fashioned herb garden that illustrates the beauty of plants jostling for space and overflowing on to pathways

Part of an informal herb garden, showing the interest, texture and form that herbs can provide

Herbs may also be planted informally in beds with other ornamental plants; a useful ploy when you do not have enough space for a separate herb garden. A charming idea is to include those herbs that will attract butterflies and bees: common or English lavender (*Lavandula angustifolia*) and pink carnation (dianthus), for instance.

Example size

6.75 (22ft) long by x 3.4m (11ft) wide. This is a large herb bed and will need to have stepping stones placed randomly within the design to give access to the herbs for harvesting and general maintenance.

A plan for an informal herb bed

Key to illustration:

1 Lovage	18 Pot marigold
2 Angelica	19 Lemon balm
3 Golden rod	20 Hyssop
4 Elecampane	21 Lavender
5 Mullein	22 Scented leaf
6 Bronze fennel	geranium
7 Southernwood	23 Thyme
8 Curry plant	24 Feverfew
9 Mint	25 Pinks
10 St John's wort	26 Chives
11 Marshmallow	27 Pennyroyal
12 Salad burnet	28 Lily of the valley
13 Poppies	29 Heartsease
14 Rue	30 Chamomile
15 Cumin	
16 Marjoram	
17 Sage	

Herb beds positioned, dug and ready for planting

Planting suggestions

Backdrop: Wall, trellis or hedge

Tall herbs

Angelica (*Angelica archangelica*): Height 1–2.5m (3–8ft), spread 45cm–1.1m (18–43in). Use one plant.

Bronze fennel (*Foeniculum vulgare* 'Purpureum'): Height 1.2–1.5m (4–5ft), spread 45cm (18in). Use one plant.

Elecampane (*Inula helenium*): Height 3m (10ft), spread 1.5m (5ft). Use one plant.

Foxglove (*Digitalis purpurea*): Height 1–2m, 2m in 2nd year (3–6ft 6in, 6ft 6in in 2nd year), spread 25cm (10in). Use five plants.

Golden rod (*Solidago virgaurea*): Height to 1.5m (5ft), spread 45–60cm (18–24in). Use three plants.

Lovage (*Levisticum officinale*): Height 2m (6ft 6in), spread 1m (39in). Use one plant.

Marsh mallow (*Althaea officinalis*): Height 1–1.2m (39–47in), spread 60–90cm (24–36in). Use one plant.

Mullein (*Verbascum thapsus*): Height 2m (6ft 6in), spread 1m (39in). Use three plants, in an uneven group.

Medium-sized herbs

Curry plant (*Helichrysum italicum* syn. *H. angustifolium*): Height 60cm (24in), spread 1m (39in). Use one plant.

English lavender (*Lavandula angustifolia*): Height and spread 60–90cm (24–36in). Use two plants.

Evening primrose (*Oenothera biennis*): Height 30cm–1.5m (1–5ft), spread 22.5–30cm (9–12in). Use five plants.

Feverfew (*Tanacetum parthenium* formerly *Chrysanthemum*): Height 60cm (24in), spread 45cm (18in). Use three plants.

Hyssop (*Hyssopus officinalis*): Height 45–60cm (18–24in), spread 60–90cm (24–36in). Use three plants.

Lemon balm (*Melissa officinalis*): Height 30–80cm (12–32in), spread 30–45cm (12–18in). Use three plants.

Rue (*Ruta graveolens*): Height 60cm (24in), spread 45cm (18in). Use three plants.

Sage (*Salvia officinalis*): Height 60–80cm (24–32in), spread 1m (39in). Use one plant.

St John's wort (*Hypericum perforatum*): Height 30–60cm (12–24in), spread 15–45cm (6–18in). Use five plants.

Salad burnet (*Sanguisorba minor*): Height to 75cm (30in), spread 30cm (12in). Use five plants.

Southernwood (*Artemisia abrotanum*): Height 1m (39in), spread 30–60cm (12–24in). Use three plants.

Spearmint (*Mentha spicata*): Height 30cm–1m (12–39in), spread indefinite. Use one plant.

Thyme (*Thymus vulgaris*): Height 30–45cm (12–18in), spread 60cm (24in). Use two plants.

Wild marjoram (*Origanum vulgare*): Height and spread 45cm (18in). Use three plants.

Plants for infilling

Borage (*Borago officinalis*): Height 30cm–1m (12–39in), spread 15–30cm (6–12in). Use five plants.

Field poppy (*Papaver rhoas*): Height 20–90cm (8–36in), spread 10–45cm (4–18in). Use five plants.

Pot marigold (*Calendula officinalis*): Height and spread 50–70cm (20–28in). Use two plants.

Scented-leaf geraniums (eg Nutmeg geranium, *Pelargonium* 'Fragrans'): Height and spread 45cm (18 in). Use four plants.

Small plants

Apple pelargonium (*Pelargonium odoratissimum*): Height 30cm (12in), spread 15–45cm (6–18in). Use
    three plants.

Cumin (*Cuminum cyminum*): Height 15–30cm (6–12in), spread 8–10cm (3–4in). Use seven plants.

German chamomile (*Matricaria recutita*): Height 15–30cm (6–24in), spread 10–38cm (4–15in). Use five.

Heartsease/wild pansies (*Viola tricolor*): Height and spread 38cm (15in). Use three plants.

Lavender (*Lavandula angustifolia* 'Nana Alba'): Height 15–30cm (6–12in), spread 15–45cm (6–18in). Use
    three plants.

Lily of the valley (*Convallaria majalis*): Height 22.5–30cm (9–12in), spread indefinite. Use two plants.

Sweet marjoram (*Origanum majorana*): Height and spread to 45cm (18in).
    Use two plants.

Edging herbs

Chives (*Allium schoenoprasum*): Height 10–60cm (4–24in), spread 30cm (12in). Use five plants.

Pennyroyal (*Mentha pulegium*): Height 10–40cm (4–16in), spread indefinite. Use one or two plants.

Pinks/carnations (eg *Dianthus chinensis* 'Strawberry Parfait'): Height and spread 20cm (8in). Use
    five plants.

Rock hyssop (*Hyssopus officinalis* subsp. *aristatus*): Height and spread 30cm (12in). Use two plants.

Thymes (eg Red-flowered thyme *Thymus serpyllum coccineus*): Height 1–7.5cm (^{1}/2–3in), spread 1m
    (39in). Use one plant.

HERB GARDEN MAINTENANCE

Once your garden is established, you will find its general upkeep and maintenance relatively easy. Usually, a weekly meander around, weeding, harvesting, clipping and dead heading more than suffices.

During the summer months, the occasional organic feed can be given. By and large, all but the moisture-loving herbs (such as sweet cicely, sorrel (*Rumex acetosa*), mint, bergamot and comfrey) will tolerate dry conditions for short periods, but all herbs do need to be watered occasionally, particularly angelica and parsley. The application of a mulch – for example chipped bark, cocoa shell, gravel or coarse grit – will help to conserve water in the soil.

Herbs need regular dead heading of flowers, and dead and shrivelled leaves need to be nipped off to deter pests and diseases.

Rotting vegetation also harbours pests and diseases, so remove it. It may also be necessary to give plants that need formal shaping several clips a year until you achieve the required shape. Cut back withered or broken branches to soil level to help strengthen the plant. Weeds are seldom a problem as herbs are rampant growers.

Annual herbs should be dug up at the end of the growing season. Perennials should be cut off at their base; stake them and write the name of each one on a marker, placing the marker close to each plant, so that you will know what is going to come up in that particular spot the following year. Evergreens should also be cut back vigorously. For winter protection in colder parts of the country, apply a layer of straw to your herb garden, beds and borders.

2 CHOOSING HERBS FOR A GARDEN

The herbs you intend to grow are a matter of personal taste although the number and size will be dictated by the space available. But whatever you grow, the cultural needs and habits of your plants must come first. So how do you go about choosing which herbs to plant? A small selection of the well-known favourites will give you a good starting point and then you can go on to build up your collection as your knowledge and expertise grow. Start with the 'big five': parsley, chives, mint, thyme and rosemary. These are all easy-care herbs that are simple to grow, will give you a useful stock, and will thrive with comparatively little effort on your part.

Parsley

Parsley, which grows to a height of 30–45cm (12–18in), is a native of central and southern Europe and is biennial, but grows better if treated as an annual. It has curled, crisp, green leaves, and the flowers, which are produced in flat sprays during the second year, are greenish-yellow. First-year plants produce finer, more succulent leaves than second-year ones.

The bright green, crimply leaved variety, *Petroselinum crispum*, is the most commonly grown form, although the seed is notoriously slow to germinate, particularly when the weather is wet, sometimes taking eight weeks.

Parsley, with its crisp, curled leaves, is a rich source of vitamin C and is best known as a culinary herb. It is a biennial and makes a good edging plant for beds and borders

Germination can be encouraged by soaking the seed in warm water and by pouring boiling water on to the soil before sowing.

In order to ensure a constant supply of this useful herb, seed should be sown twice a year: in early spring, for a summer crop, and again in mid-summer for winter use.

Parsley likes a fairly rich, non-acid, well-drained soil with plenty of moisture. A certain amount of sun is important, but the herb will only grow well when its roots are cool, so it should be shaded for part of the day. Dig the soil thoroughly, rake to a fine tilth, and sow the seed thinly in rows 30cm (12in) apart, covering them lightly with soil. When large enough to handle, the seedlings should be pricked out to a distance of 20cm (8in). Handle carefully to prevent injury to the roots which could cause the plants to run to seed. Parsley can also be grown in pots: see Chapter 4, page 63.

Parsley should be kept free from weeds and watered liberally during periods of dry weather. Cut out the flowering stems during the second year – the plant dies after producing seed – to encourage the production of leaves and to lengthen the period of useful life. Pick the foliage regularly, leaving only the green centre of the plant. If you intend to harvest your own seed, leave a few of the plants to flower.

Chives

Chives (*Allium schoenoprasum*) are perennial bulbous plants, and with their pretty, clover-like, pinkish-purple flowers that appear in early to mid-summer and their grass-like foliage, they make lovely garden plants in their own right. The tubular leaves, which grow to a height of 23–30cm (9–12in), are evergreen in most climates, but can die back completely in less mild winters.

Chives are easy to grow. Seed can be sown outdoors in spring in drills 25cm (10in) apart and the seedlings thinned to about 15cm (6in) apart. Seed sown outside usually takes in excess of two weeks to germinate. Seed can also be planted in trays in the greenhouse or directly into pots. Germination under glass at 21°C (70°F) will take around six days. Chive seedlings grow as small, white bulbs with a thin, tapering, green shoot protruding from them. This small bulb produces new bulbs, so several seedlings can be planted together without fear of overcrowding. Chives like a rich, moist but well-drained soil and they also prefer a little shade. Chives grow in clumps and should be divided every two or three years in spring. Always water well after replanting and trim the tops to encourage the growth of new leaves. Remove the flowers to encourage leaf production.

Chives are hardy perennials that will grow in some shade and can be grown in tubs and pots

Spearmint is a common culinary mint

Mint

There are many different varieties of mints, the best known ones being: applemint (*Mentha suaveolens*), Bowles mint (*M. rotundifolia*), Eau de Cologne mint (*M. x piperita* 'Citrata'), peppermint (*M. piperita*) and spearmint (*M. spicata*). All mints have a strong, aromatic smell, grow rapidly and spread by underground runners, making them very invasive. They need plenty of water when growing and they also need to be kept firmly under control. They are best planted in a bottomless bucket or pot which has been sunk into the soil up to its rim (see page 54). Mints are good for container planting as they are so invasive; planting in pots keeps them under control.

Mints are perennials that can be grown from seed or from root divisions. They can

have ovate, lanceolate or ovate-lanceolate leaves and lilac, pink or white flowers. They prefer a moist, rich soil in a shady place, but will grow almost anywhere. Plant different varieties well apart to avoid cross-flavouring.

When it comes to flavour, there are really just two types: peppermint and spearmint. Peppermint has long, hairy, purplish-green leaves, while spearmint, probably the best known of the culinary mints, has narrow, pointed, green leaves and lilac flowers. It usually grows to around 30–40cm (12–16in) in height.

Thyme

There are many varieties of thyme, but *Thymus vulgaris* is the garden or common thyme most often seen in gardens. It is a small, aromatic, shrubby evergreen, hardy perennial herb, growing up to 45cm (18in) in height. It has woody stems, small, dark green leaves and pale mauve flowers that appear in early summer. It likes a light, well-drained, gravelly soil and a sunny, warm position. It can easily be raised from seed sown in spring. Press the seed into the surface of the compost in a seed tray and transplant the seedlings to 30–45cm (12–18in) apart when large enough to handle. Thymes are ideal for planting in pots.

Propagation is from cuttings taken in mid-summer with a 'heel' attached, which are then rooted in pots of sandy soil in a cold frame (see page 48). Tip cuttings can be taken in summer and the plants can also be divided in spring. Alternatively, plants can be layered. Cut the plants well back in mid-summer, and in autumn to free them of old wood and keep them bushy. Shelter from the cold and wind is important. Thyme is unlikely to survive a hard winter, although it can withstand drought in summer.

Garden thyme (*Thymus vulgaris*) is most useful in the kitchen

Rosemary

Rosemary (*Rosmarinus officinalis*) is a perennial, evergreen shrub with long, spiky leaves and a pungent, aromatic scent. Its small, pale blue flowers start to appear in late winter if the weather is mild, and continue until late spring.

It will grow outdoors to a height of 2m (6ft 6in) in a sheltered spot, and prefers a light, well-drained soil, with the benefit of some lime – try sprinkling some crushed egg shells around it – in a sunny position. It will grow well against a wall, often growing taller, although it tends to grow sideways once it has reached its maximum height.

Rosemary is difficult to cultivate from seed, but if you are successful the plants will be better than those raised from cuttings.

Seed sown in trays under glass in mid- to late spring will produce decent plants by autumn. The seed can also be planted in shallow drills in mid- to late spring. Plants can be grown from 'soft', not woody, cuttings taken from strong side shoots from early spring to early autumn. The rooted cuttings can be over-wintered in the greenhouse.

Rosemary is hardy except in severe weather conditions and wet soil; cold, frosty weather can destroy it completely. It is extremely decorative and can be planted as a single specimen. It also makes a good hedge, and can be grown in a pot.

Rosemary can be grown in a large pot, or makes a good hedge if clipped after flowering

EFFORTLESS ANNUALS AND BIENNIALS

Annuals

Annuals and those herbs which self-seed (treated as annuals for the purpose of cultivation) are grown from seed each spring.

Biennials

Biennials are grown from seed and are so called because they take two years to complete their life cycle. Usually, they flower and produce seed during the second year, but it is possible to keep them growing as perennials for several years simply by removing their flower heads. You can, of course, allow some of the plants to set their seed and produce seedlings, after which you can select the strongest ones and plant them in a position suited to their needs.

Caraway, a biennial, flowers in its second year

Many herbs are very decorative, as well as useful for culinary purposes

Common annual herbs

Anise (*Pimpinella anisum*)
Basil (*Ocimum basilicum*)
Borage (*Borago officinalis*)
Chervil (*Anthriscus cerefolium*)
Common balsam (*Impatiens balsamina*)
Coriander (*Coriandrum sativum*)
Dill (*Anethum graveolens* also
　　　Peucedanum graveolens)
Nasturtium (*tropaeolum*)
Rocket (*Eruca vesicaria* subsp. *sativa*)
Summer savoury (*Satureja hortensis*)
Sunflower (*Helianthus annuus*)
Sweet marjoram (*Origanum majorana*)

Common biennial herbs

Angelica (*Angelica archangelica*)
Caraway (*Carum carvi*)
Clary sage (*Salvia sclarea*)
Cotton thistle (*Onopordon acanthium*)
Evening primrose (*Oenothera biennis*)
Mullein (*Verbascum thapsus*)
Parsley (*Petroselinum crispum*), usually treated
　　　as an annual
Viper's bugloss (*Echium vulgare*)

PERENNIALS

Perennials are a large group of herbs that live for several years or more. Some of them can be grown from seed, although they may take three to four weeks to germinate when sown under glass in early spring. Many of them also grow well when sown in late summer or early autumn as soon as the seeds are ripe: sweet cicely and lovage, for example.

Most perennial herbs are either shrubs or herbaceous perennials (those we consider more for their visual effect). They are generally sold in pots for planting directly where they are to grow. Shrubby perennials, such as bay, rosemary and sage, should be planted out in early spring or late autumn in humus-rich soil.

Once perennial herbs are established, many of them can be increased by division – chives, for instance – or, as in the case of mint, by root runners. Perennial herbs can be propagated by several methods, including cuttings, and, if you increase your own stock in this way, you will not have to buy potted perennials, which will cut down your expenses considerably.

In moderate and cold climates, most perennial herbs will die back at the end of the summer and virtually disappear into the soil, their root systems remaining underground. If you live in a cold area, protect your plants over winter with a layer of organic mulch (such as spent mushroom compost, seaweed, dried lawn clippings or garden compost). Such mulches will not only protect them from frosts, but will also provide nutrients valuable to them. In spring, the herbs will reappear and should be mulched again to encourage leaf growth and later flowers.

Tansy is an invasive perennial that is very easy to grow. If it self-seeds, tiny plants will appear everywhere

Common perennial herbs

Fennel (*Foeniculum vulgare*)
Hyssop (*Hyssopus officinalis*)
Lemon balm (*Melissa officinalis*)
Rue (*Ruta graveolens*)
Sweet cicely (*Myrrhis odorata*)
Tansy (*Tanacetum vulgare*)

Lemon balm is a useful ingredient of potpourri

Fennel needs plenty of room to grow

HERBS FOR SHADE

Many herbs will grow in either sunny or shady places. A shady part of the garden, under a tree, for example, hardly seems conducive to growing herbs, but, in actual fact, there are many herbs, particularly those with medicinal uses, that will tolerate or even prefer shade.

Herbs grown in shade do flower, but their blooms are often of poor quality, and they also usually flower very early in the year. Shade reduces the range of herbs that you can grow, but there is a wide variety of culinary, ornamental and other herbs that will flourish in shady spots.

A heavily shaded herb patch will most happily have woodland perennials as its inmates. It will be at its brightest from late winter to early spring. The first to flower will be the woodland hellebores (helleborus) and the herb lungwort (*Pulmonaria officinalis*), followed by violet and woodruff, then lily of the valley, Jacob's ladder (*Polemonium caeruleum*) and Solomon's seal (*Polygonatum multiflorum*).

Lungwort or pulmonaria appears early in spring

Herbs for heavy shade

Evening primrose (*Oenothera biennis*)

Lily of the valley (*Convallaria majalis*)

Pennyroyal (*Mentha pulegium*)

Sweet violet (*Viola odorata*)

Valerian (*Valeriana officinalis*)

Woodruff (*Galium odoratum*)

Herbs enjoying damp shade

Some herbs enjoy a position with damp shade: ginger mint (*Mentha* x *gracilis* 'Variegata'), for example. Given these conditions, ginger mint will bear long, red stems with lilac flowers between its green and gold leaves from early summer to autumn. Both creeping pennyroyal (*Mentha pulegium* 'Cunningham Mint') and upright pennyroyal (*Mentha pulegium*) will become a carpet of scented leaves along paths and banks, and other herbs such as elecampane (*Inula helenium*) and bugle (*Ajuga reptans*) will flourish in a moist, shady position.

Herbs for partial shade

There are other herbs that will flower later and prefer a dappled shade: angelica, for example. Lovage also prefers some shade to develop its large leaves, and sorrel thrives in shade, producing better leaves in consequence. Light or gold variegated herbs such as golden marjoram, golden sage and variegated lemon balm prefer dappled shade, and they also benefit from the sun not scorching their foliage. Chervil is also fond of shady places, as is borage.

Other herbs for partial shade

Figwort (*Scrophularia nodosa*)

Foxglove (*Digitalis purpurea*)

Lady's mantle (*Alchemilla mollis*)

Musk mallow (*Malva moschata*)

Rocket (*Eruca vesicaria* subsp. *sativa*)

St John's wort (*Hypericum perforatum*)

Sweet cicely (*Myrrhis odorata*)

Wild honeysuckle (*Lonicera periclymenum*)

Ginger mint will flower readily in damp shade

Borage enjoys a shady position

TALL AND MEDIUM HERBS

There is a whole range of architectural, statuesque herbs which are ideal for the herbaceous border. When planning a herb border, plant the tallest herbs at the back in clumps rather than in rows for a cottage garden effect. If planting an island bed that can be viewed from all round, plant them in the centre to prevent them from overshadowing the smaller plants. Tall herbs can be slotted in anywhere in the garden, to hide a fence or wall, or placed in the vegetable garden, for example. Bear in mind that tall herbs need plenty of space around them, so allow about 60cm (2ft) between them when planting.

Foxgloves look majestic at the back of a border

Yellow-flowering mullein grows to 1.5m (5ft)

Common tall herbs

Angelica (*Angelica archangelica*) can reach 1.2–1.8m (4–6ft)

Chicory (*Cichorium intybus*) will grow to 1.2m (4ft) but usually needs staking

Elecampane (*Inula helenium*) can reach 1.2–1.8m (4–6ft)

Fennel (*Foeniculum vulgare*), which will grow to 1.5m (5ft), shouldn't need support because of its upright habit.

Lovage (*Levisticum officinale*), can reach 1.2–1.8m (4–6ft); may need staking despite its strong, upright growth

Mullein (*Verbascum thapsus*) will grow to 1.5m (5ft)

If space permits, you might include
Bay (*Laurus nobilis*)
Foxglove (*Digitalis purpurea*)
Jacob's ladder (*Polemonium caeruleum*)
Soapwort (*Saponaria officinalis*)
Wormwood (*Artemisia absinthium*)

Herbs of medium height

Agrimony (*Agrimonia eupatoria*)

Basil (*Ocimum basilicum*)

Borage (*Borago officinalis*)

Caraway (*Carum carvi*)

Comfrey (*Symphytum officinale*)

Coriander (*Coriandrum sativum*)

Cotton lavender (*Santolina chamaecyparissus*)

Curry plant (*Helichrysum italicum* syn.
    H. angustifolium)

Dill (*Anethum graveolens* also *Peucedanum graveolens*)

Feverfew (*Tanacetum parthenium* formerly
    Chrysanthemum)

Horehound (*Marrubium vulgare*)

Hyssop (*Hyssopus officinalis*)

Lavender (lavandula)

Lemon balm (*Melissa officinalis*)

Mint (mentha)

Marjoram (origanum)

Pot marjoram (*Origanum onites*)

Rampion (*Campanula rapunculus*)

Rue (*Ruta graveolens*)

Sages (salvia)

St John's wort (*Hypericum perforatum*)

Sorrel (*Rumex acetosa*)

Southernwood (*Artemisia abrotanum*)

Sweet cicely (*Myrrhis odorata*)

Tansy (*Tanacetum vulgare*)

Valerian (*Valeriana officinalis*)

Tarragon (*Artemisia dracunculus*)

Viper's bugloss (*Echium vulgare*)

Winter savory (*Satureja montana*)

Sorrel is a useful plant for the middle of a herb border, or even a flower bed

Golden feverfew is a beautiful, decorative herb that grows to a height of about 45cm (18in)

LOW-GROWING HERBS

Low-growing herbs are best located in the front of the garden where they will get plenty of sun. They are also useful for edging beds or paths. You might like to try the white flowering lavender *Lavandula angustifolia* 'Nana Alba', which is very low-growing, reaching a height of 15–30cm (6–12in). To enclose a herb garden, a hedge of clipped box is neat and attractive, as is lavender. One of the best varieties of lavender for hedging is *Lavandula angustifolia* 'Royal Purple', with its deep purple flowers and compact habit, growing to a height of 80cm (32in).

Paths can be softened by cascading thymes, chamomile, Corsican mint (*Mentha requienii*) and creeping winter savory (*Satureja spicigera*). Pennyroyal and sweet marjoram are also low-growing, although their flower stems can rise above the main level of the plant.

Chives and parsley make attractive edges for beds and borders, and rock hyssop (*Hyssopus officinalis* subsp. *aristatus*) is ideal for planting in paving or for rock gardens as it only grows to 20–30cm (8–12in) tall.

Low-growing Corsican mint

Low-growing plants: to 45cm (18in)

Perennials
Bistort (*Polygonum bistorta*)
Calamint (*Calamintha officinalis*)
Chives (*Allium schoenoprasum*)
Double chamomile (*Chamaemelum nobile* 'Flore Pleno')
Sweet marjoram (*Origanum majorana*)
Thyme (thymus)
Winter savory (*Satureja montana*)

Annuals and biennials
Anise (*Pimpinella anisum*)
Basils (ocimum)
Cumin (*Cuminum cyminum*)
Parsley (*Petroselinum crispum*)

PROSTRATE HERBS

Prostrate herbs grow rampantly to produce a dense carpet of foliage and often a mass of flowers as well. They can be used to cover unsightly areas of bare earth, to suppress weeds and to soften any harsh features. They are very effective in the herb garden, and there are varieties of prostrate herbs for both sunny and shady areas. There are also many suitable for paths, but they need to be enclosed by small pieces of brick or slate to prevent them encroaching on the herb beds.

Creeping thyme (*Thymus serpyllum*) will cover paths and paving slabs with a scented carpet of flowers and foliage. It will soften cracks, smother banks and thrive on the tops of walls.

Corsican mint (*Mentha requienii*) will flourish under shrubs and trees, as will woodland herbs such as woodruff (*Galium odoratum*) with its spreading mass of starry, white flowers.

HERB THEMES

Over the centuries, herbs have been used in many different ways, all of which provide an open-ended source of ideas for herb themes, which can range from a Biblical Herb Garden to one that grows salad herbs. Herbs adapt to a number of themes and designs, but whatever you decide upon, always establish where your garden is going to be sited and always plan it to scale on paper before you start.

POTPOURRI GARDEN

Plant a potpourri garden and you will have the scents of summer all winter long. Try growing peonies for their strong red flowers and pinks for their truly wonderful scent. Lavender also makes a lovely aromatic addition, as does Eau de Cologne mint that goes so well with the lemon herbs. Violets are ideal for their perfume and colour as is lemon balm with its clean fresh smell. And, as a backdrop to this type of garden, grow wonderfully fragrant roses and sweetly scented honeysuckle.

Potpourri garden planting suggestions

Alecost (*Tanacetum balsaminta*)
Bergamot (*Monarda didyma*)
Borage (*Borago officinalis*)
Carnations (*Dianthus chinensis* 'Strawberry Parfait')
Catmint (*Nepeta cataria*)
German chamomile (*Matricaria recutita*)
Ginger mint (*Mentha x gracilis* 'Variegata')
Japanese honeysuckle (*Lonicera japonica*)
Lavender (lavandula)
Lemon balm (*Melissa officinalis*)
Lemon verbena (*Aloysia triphylla*)
Pennyroyal (*Mentha pulegium*)
Peony (*Paeonia officinalis*)
Pineapple sage (*Salvia elegans* 'Scarlet Pineapple')
Rose, climbing (*Rosa* 'Rosy Mantle')
Rosemary (*Rosmarinus officinalis*)
Scented leaf geraniums (pelargonium)
Southernwood (*Artemisia abrotanum*)
Thyme (thymus)
Variegated lemon balm (*Melissa officinalis* 'Aurea')
Violets (*Viola odorata*)

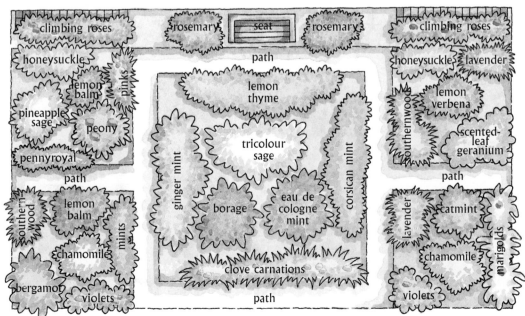

A ground plan of a potpourri garden

DYER'S GARDEN

If you are interested in spinning and weaving and dyeing your own wools, what better than to have your own dye herbs so that you can mix your own colours?

The petals of pot marigold produce a pale yellow dye, earning it a place in a dyer's garden

Common gypsyweed or gipsywort (*Lycopus europaeus*) will yield a brown dye

Dyer's garden planting suggestions

For reds
Dyer's bugloss (*Alkanna tinctoria*)
Dyer's madder roots (*Rubia tinctorum*)
Lady's bedstraw (*Galium verum*)
Rue (*Ruta graveolens*)
Sorrel (*Rumex acetosa*)

For blues
Berries of the elder tree (*Sambucus nigra*)
Berries of privet (*Ligustrum vulgare*)
Woad leaves (*Ivatis tinctoria*)
Indigo (*Indigofera tinctoria*)
Berries of juniper (*Juniperus communis*)

For greens
Ivy (*Hedera helix*)
Lily of the valley (*Convallaria majalis*)
Nettles (*Urtica urens*)
St John's wort (*Hypericum perforatum*)
Tansy (*Tanacetum vulgare*)

For bright yellows
Agrimony (*Agrimonia eupatoria*)
Broom (*Cytisus scoparius*)
Golden rod (*Solidago virgaurea*)
Lily of the valley (*Convallaria majalis*)
Tansy flowers (*Tanacetum vulgare*)
Thyme (*thymus*)

For softer yellows
Apples (*Malus sylvestris* var. *domestica*)
Daffodil (*narcissus*)
Dandellon (*Taraxacum officinale*)
Pears (*Pyrus communis* var. *sativa*)
Pot marigold (*Calendula officinalis*)

For black
Roots of meadowsweet (*Filipendula ulmaria*)

MEDICINAL GARDEN

Medicinal herbs were widely used in the past, but no one should ever attempt to treat themselves with any medicinal herbs without first seeking advice from a qualified herbalist.

The number and variety of herbs that you plant will depend on the size of the garden. Do not overcrowd the beds.

Tall herbs are planted towards the centre as the garden will be viewed from all sides.

Plan of a medicinal herb garden

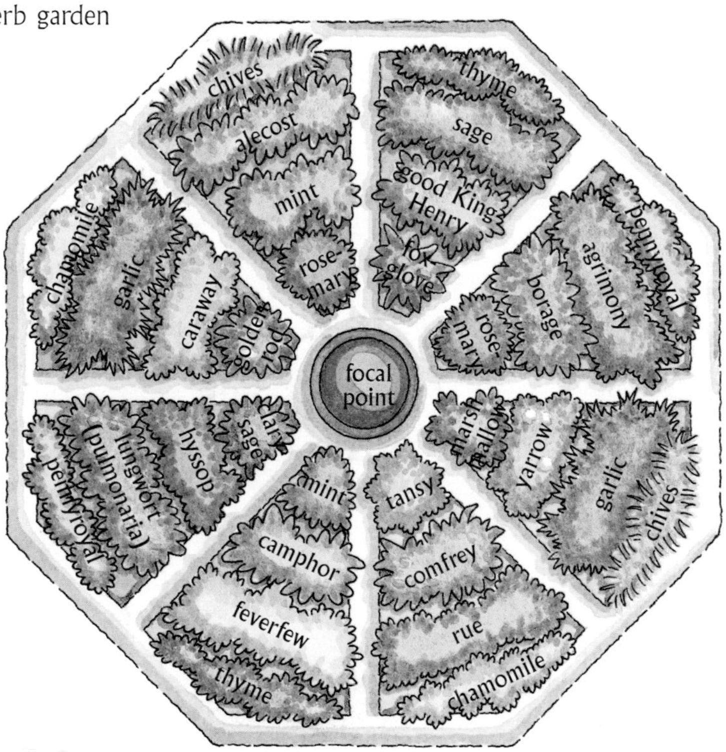

Medicinal garden planting suggestions

Agrimony (*Agrimonia eupatoria*)

Borage (*Borago officinalis*)

Caraway (*Carum carvi*)

Catmint (*Nepeta cataria*)

Chives (*Allium schoenoprasum*)

Clary sage (*Salvia sclarea*)

Comfrey (*Symphytum officinale*)

Feverfew (*Tanacetum parthenium* formerly *Chrysanthemum*)

Foxglove (*Digitalis purpurea*)

Garlic (*Allium sativum*)

German chamomile (*Matricaria recutita*)

Golden rod (*Solidago virgaurea*)

Good King Henry (*Chenopodium bonus–henricus*)

Hyssop (*Hyssopus officinalis*)

Lungwort (*Pulmonaria officinalis*)

Marsh mallow (*Althaea officinalis*)

Mints (*mentha*)

Pennyroyal (*Mentha pulegium*)

Rosemary (*Rosmarinus officinalis*)

Rue (*Ruta graveolens*)

Sages (*salvia*)

Tansy (*Tanacetum vulgare*)

Thymes (*thymus*)

TEA GARDEN

Growing herbs to make herbal teas or tisanes is not difficult. They make delicious drinks served hot, cold or iced. Some are slightly stimulating, many are tonics. They are a pleasant alternative to tea and coffee and don't contain tannin or caffeine. Before drinking a herbal tea, always check with a qualified herbal practitioner, as people suffering from certain medical conditions should not drink particular teas.

Plan of a tea garden

Tea garden planting suggestions

Angelica (*Angelica archangelica*)
Fennel (*Foeniculum vulgare*)
Hyssop (*Hyssopus officinalis*)
Lemon balm (*Melissa officinalis*)
Lemon verbena (*Aloysia triphylla*)
Mints (mentha)
  Ginger mint (*M. x gracilis* 'Variegata')
  Peppermint (*M. piperita*)
Rosemary (*Rosmarinus officinalis*)
Sages (salvia)
Thymes (thymus)

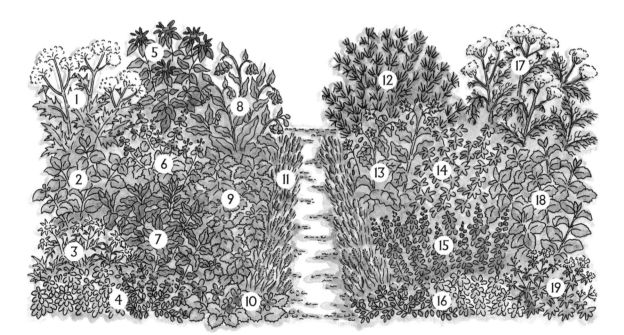

Key to illustration:	10	Violets
1 Angelica	11	Lavender
2 Basil	12	Rosemary
3 Chamomile	13	Borage
4 Thymes	14	Lemon verbena
5 Bergamot	15	Hyssop
6 Ginger mint	16	Thymes
7 Sage	17	Fennel
8 Comfrey	18	Peppermint
9 Lemon balm	19	Woodruff

EVERLASTING HERB GARDEN

There are many herbs that can be successfully harvested and dried, in order to bring their rich scents and colours into the house during the long winter months. The following selection of herbs will remind you of summer days and, when dried (see pages 147–51), they can all be used in flower arrangements. They dry easily, retaining both their shape and colour.

Everlasting garden planting suggestions

Bergamot (*Monarda didyma*)

Borage (*Borago officinalis*)

Cotton lavender (*Santolina chamaecyparissus*)

Hops (*Humulus lupulus*)

Lavender (*lavandula*)

Love-in-the-mist (*Nigella damascena*)

Poppies (*papaver*)

Purple leaved sage (*Salvia officinalis* 'Purpurascens')

Rosemary (*Rosmarinus officinalis*)

Safflower (*Carthamus tinctorius*)

Tansy (*Tanacetum vulgare*)

Dog rose (*Rosa canina*) adds colour to any garden

SHAKESPEAREAN HERB GARDEN

The Elizabethans valued herbs very highly and Shakespeare mentioned them frequently in his plays. He wrote of 'hot lavender' and 'rosemary for remembrance', as well as rue which he called 'the sour herb of grace'.

Heartsease was popular in Shakespearean times

Shakespearean garden planting suggestions

Bay (*Laurus nobilis*)

Caraway (*Carum carvi*)

Chamomile, lawn (*Chamaemelum nobile* 'Treneague')

Cowslip (*Primula veris*)

Fennel (*Foeniculum vulgare*)

Heartsease (*Viola tricolor*)

Iris (*Iris florentina*)

Lavender (*lavandula*)

Lemon balm (*Melissa officinalis*)

Marjoram (*origanum*)

Myrtle (*Myrtus communis*)

Parsley (*Petroselinum crispum*)

Pinks (*dianthus*)

Rose (*rosa*)

Rosemary (*Rosmarinus officinalis*)

Rue (*Ruta graveolens*)

Salad burnet (*Sanguisorba minor*)

Savory (*satureja*)

Thyme, creeping (*Thymus serpyllum*)

Violet (*Viola odorata*)

Wild honeysuckle (*Lonicera periclymenum*)

Wormwood (*Artemisia absinthium*)

3 PROPAGATION, PRUNING, PESTS AND DISEASES

GROWING FROM SEED

Many herbs can be raised from seed, although there are some exceptions. Tarragon, for instance, rarely sets seed and has to be propagated by means of its creeping underground stems.

Growing from seed gives you a greater variety of plants, is much cheaper, and allows you to experiment with different species. (Obviously, if you only need one plant, then it's more economical to buy it.) You don't need a greenhouse to grow seed, but if you have one, so much the better, as it provides a protected environment that will allow you to over-winter plants and to encourage tender seedlings into early growth.

All seed should be as fresh as possible if you are to be sure that it is going to germinate and sprout. It is therefore worth considering buying your seed from a mail-order catalogue rather than from a local garden centre where it may not have been stored in ideal conditions. National seed suppliers provide the freshest seeds possible.

Some herbs to grow from seed

All annual herbs are raised from seed, as are biennials.

Among the perennials worth growing from seed are:

Fennel (*Foeniculum vulgare*)

Feverfew (*Tanacetum parthenium* formerly *Chrysanthemum*)

Lovage (*Levisticum officinale*)

Marsh mallow (*Althaea officinalis*)

Oregano, also known as wild marjoram (*Origanum vulgare*)

Dill bears umbels of yellow flowers in summer

Nasturtium seeds can be pickled and eaten

ANNUALS
Sowing seed directly into soil

Hardy annuals are easy to grow because they can be planted where they are to flower. Sow seed directly into the prepared soil in spring and thin according to the directions on the seed packet. Borage, chervil, dill, coriander and summer savory are all hardy annuals that can be treated in this way. Or why not try pot marigolds or poppies which will provide wonderful splurges of colour?

STAGE 1: Make sure that your site has been well dug and is free from weeds and stones. Rake the soil level, breaking up any clumps of earth, until a fine tilth is obtained.

STAGE 2: Using a hoe, make shallow drills 6mm (¼in) deep at a spacing according to the variety of herb. Sow the seed as evenly as possible along the drills. It's a good idea to pour it into a dish and to scatter it a pinch at a time, using your thumb and forefinger.

STAGE 3: Label each variety and the date when sown, then rake the soil level to cover the seed.

STAGE 4: Water in dry weather until the seed is well established.

STAGE 5: Thin the seedlings according to the requirements of the variety, leaving them spaced at the distance recommended on the seed packet.

Broadcast sowing

If you intend to plant groups of one type of herb, then the seed can be sown broadcast.

STAGE 1: Scatter the seed over the designated area as evenly as possible.

Annual poppies are grown for their vibrant colour

STAGE 2: Rake it in, first in one direction, then at right-angles.

STAGE 3: Thin the seedlings as before and keep well watered in dry weather.

Sowing in pots or cold frame

Hardy annuals sown in pots or in a cold frame in autumn flower earlier than those sown outside. They can be hardened off and planted to fill any gaps in the herb garden or border.

Many of the annuals can be sown a month or so earlier if you have a greenhouse or cold frame, and these will be ready to plant out once the danger of frost is over; later sowings will give a succession of colour throughout the year.

STAGE 1: Sow seed thinly on moistened compost in seed trays in a gentle heat in late winter or early spring. Fine seed should be pressed down lightly with a piece of wood, larger seeds being covered with a thin layer of compost. Sow one variety per tray.

STAGE 2: Label each variety clearly and add the date.

STAGE 3: Cover the trays with clear plastic, glass or polythene. Place newspaper on top to eliminate light.

STAGE 4: When the seedlings appear – about one week later, depending upon the variety – remove the newspaper and coverings.

STAGE 5: Prick out the seedlings when they have two pairs of leaves.

STAGE 6: When large enough, harden them off. Plant them out in their permanent growing positions in late spring or early summer, when all danger of frost has passed.

Many of the annuals only take two or three months to flower, and those planted out at the beginning of summer will be ready for harvesting at the end of it. Borage and summer savory are two of the herbs that ripen particularly quickly, and borage will self-seed freely.

Seeds germinate faster in a greenhouse where they can be sown in trays in early spring. Some seeds need a period of cold before they will germinate – angelica, juniper (*Juniperus communis*), sweet violet, sweet cicely, woodruff, for example – while others need a higher temperature. If you sow too early, you will have to provide heat while the seedlings develop, and there will also be a problem with light levels – seedlings need the correct amount of light to sustain healthy growth. Many herb seeds will germinate within days at a constant temperature of 20–21°C (68–70°F). Turn the seed trays regularly to stop the seedlings being drawn towards the light.

Sweet violets germinate after a period of cold

Keep the plants in the greenhouse until the weather is good, shading them from strong sunlight to prevent overheating. Harden them off by standing them outside during the day and bringing them in at night. Alternatively, they can be placed in a cold frame or under a cloche, and, once all danger of frost has passed, they can then be planted out at the recommended planting distances.

HYGIENE

Keep everything clean to avoid the risk of disease. Always use clean containers, clean compost and clean seed trays. Use fresh, clean water from the tap and remember to wash out your watering can regularly. Discarded compost will encourage insect pests and the fungi that cause damping-off disease (see page 57), so keep bags of compost closed and clear up any spills. Before starting off your seeds, clean out the greenhouse and use a pesticide smoke canister in it.

HARVESTING YOUR OWN SEED

It's a good idea to allow some of your herbs to set seed rather than dead heading all of them. The seed heads can then be collected and the seeds removed and sown to raise new plants for your herb garden. Collect the seed heads – some of them in autumn, some of them earlier, depending on the herb – in a paper bag, label them, and then store them in a cool, dry, dark place ready for sowing the following spring. Alternatively, collect the seed heads as soon as they are ripe, remove the seeds and store them in labelled envelopes for ease of planting later.

Bear in mind, though, that most cultivars do not 'come true' (that is, they are not exactly the same as the parent plant) from collected seed: poppies, pot marigolds and foxgloves, for example. Usually, they produce just a percentage of plants that resemble the parent, and this percentage decreases each year with each subsequent generation of

Herb seed suitable for collection

Angelica (*Angelica archangelica*)
This seed only remains viable for about three months, so it's a good idea to plant it soon after harvesting
Borage (*Borago officinalis*)
Caraway (*Carum carvi*)
Coriander (*Coriandrum sativum*)
Jacob's ladder (*Polemonium caeruleum*)
Pot marigold (*Calendula officinalis*)
Sweet cicely (*Myrrhis odorata*)

plants. Very few variegated cultivars come true, and certain herbs may cross-pollinate and their seedlings differ from the parent plant: various kinds of thyme (thymus) marjoram (origanum) and mint (mentha) are examples. Dill and fennel will also cross-pollinate if grown near each other.

Caraway seed heads ready for harvesting. Do not allow the seed heads to become over-ripe

GROWING FROM CUTTINGS

Cuttings are the usual form of propagation for perennial herbs such as cotton lavender, rosemary and lavender. They are taken from healthy, established plants during the growing season (not when they are dormant), and there are three main types of stem cuttings: softwood, semi-ripe and hardwood. Heel and root cuttings can also be taken.

SOFTWOOD CUTTINGS

Softwood cuttings are best taken in late spring or early summer. They are taken from new shoots that have not yet hardened and from herbs that root quickly, as softwood cuttings do not survive for long without roots.

Taking softwood cuttings

STAGE 1: Select strong, non-flowering shoots with plenty of leaves and cut off 5–10cm (2–4in) of the shoot tip. Cut cleanly through the stem with a sharp knife just below a leaf node. Trim off the heel if it is ragged. Angle the cut to give a larger surface for root growth. Take several cuttings this way.

STAGE 2: Put the cuttings into a polythene bag and place in the shade until ready for use to prevent them from wilting.

Some herbs to grow from cuttings

Curry plant (*Helichrysum italicum* syn.
    H. angustifolium)
Hyssop (*Hyssopus officinalis*)
Lavender (*lavandula*)
Lemon verbena (*Aloysia triphylla*)
Marjorams (*origanum*)
Myrtle (*Myrtus communis*)
Rosemary (*Rosmarinus officinalis*)
Rue (*Ruta graveolens*)
Sages (*salvia*)
Scented-leaf geraniums (*pelargonium*)
Tarragon (*Artemisia dracunculus*)
Thymes (*thymus*)
Winter savory (*Satureja montana*)
Wormwood (*Artemisia absinthium*)

You will need:
Sharp knife
Polythene bags
Bowl of water
Hormone rooting compound
Dibber
Plant pots
Mixture of sharp sand, and peat or
    loam-based compost

STAGE 3: When ready, take out the cuttings and, with a knife, cut the leaves from the lower third so that the stems do not tear.

Choosing a suitable shoot of rosemary

Inserting cuttings around the edge of a pot

STAGE 4: Dip the cuttings in water, and then in a hormone rooting compound to one-third of their depth.

STAGE 5: Using a dibber, plant the cuttings around the edge of a flower pot filled with a mixture of sharp sand and compost.

STAGE 6: Firm them in gently, keeping the compost as loose as possible.

STAGE 7: Label, date and cover with a polythene bag.

STAGE 8: Place in a cool spot for 24 hours to allow any cuttings that may have drooped to recover. Then introduce to heat.

STAGE 9: Transplant when there is a good show of roots into their permanent growing positions.

Semi-ripe cuttings

Semi-ripe cuttings are taken from sideshoots of the current season's growth in mid- to late summer when the shoots have started to harden at the base where they join the parent plant. Select sturdy, non-flowering shoots about 5–10cm (2–4in) long. Strip the lower leaves away from the cuttings, leaving a short length of clear stem. Dip the cuttings in water and then in a hormone rooting powder. Semi-ripe cuttings taken from hardy herbs will root outside in summer. Make a slit in the soil with a trowel and insert the cuttings into it, making sure that they are not touching. Firm them in, water and label. Make sure that they are watered regularly.

Alternatively, semi-ripe cuttings will do well in a cold frame, out of the direct sun. This method of propagation is suitable for shrubby herbs such as bay and lavender.

Heel cuttings

Heel cuttings, which are vigorous sideshoots of the current season's growth, are taken from semi-ripe stems. Tear them away from the main stem with a small heel of older wood attached. Plant as for softwood cuttings. The compost should be kept moist, but there is no need to supply the humid conditions required by softwood cuttings.

Tear sideshoots away from the main stem

Hardwood cuttings

Taking hardwood cuttings is a more unusual way of propagating herbs, but again, shrubby types of herbs such as myrtle, bay and rosemary are ideal subjects. Hardwood cuttings are taken in mid- to late autumn.

STAGE 1: Select well-ripened shoots of the current season's growth, 22.5–38cm (9–15in) long, depending upon the species.

STAGE 2: Cut off any soft top growth and make a straight cut across the stem, just below a leaf node.

STAGE 3: Make a second cut 15cm (6in) above the first and above a node. Cut it at an angle. This will tell you which is the top and which is the bottom of the cutting.

STAGE 4: Moisten the base of the cutting and dip it into a hormone rooting powder.

STAGE 5: Insert the cuttings to half their length into a slit trench in open ground.

STAGE 6: Firm the cuttings in with your heel. Water in well, and label. The cuttings will gradually develop roots over winter. They can then be transplanted to their permanent locations.

Alternatively, in areas where winters are severe, plant them in a box of moist sand and store in a cool place.

Root cuttings

Herbs such as bergamot, comfrey and horseradish can be increased from thick pieces of root 5–7.5cm (2–3in) long. Cut the root and insert the pieces vertically in potting compost. Cover with a shallow layer of sand.

Mint, which has running roots, can be lifted in autumn and a few of its roots removed, cut into pieces and placed horizontally in a compost-filled tray. Cover them with a thin layer of compost and place in a cold frame where they will soon start to produce shoots.

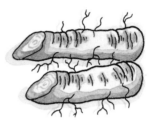

Thick root cuttings are used to propagate herbs such as bergamot, comfrey and horseradish

Insert thick root cuttings vertically in a tray of potting compost

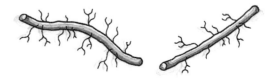

Mint can be increased from thin root cuttings

LAYERING

If cuttings are difficult to root, try layering, which can be done throughout the growing season, and is the easiest way of increasing numbers of both woody and soft-stemmed perennial herbs.

Many herbs, that grow near to the ground – thyme, for example – propagate by natural layering when a stem lying along the ground sends out roots into the surrounding soil where it touches. Layering encourages new sections of a plant to root while they are still attached to the parent plant.

Lemon balm, hyssop, marjoram, mints, horehound, curry plant, rosemary, sages, cotton lavender, violets and pinks are all suitable plants for the technique of layering.

You will usually get larger plants from layering than you would from cuttings.

STAGE 2: Dip the cut in some hormone rooting powder.

STAGE 3: Make a shallow drill where the stem will touch the soil. Dig in some compost and some fine grit.

STAGE 4: Bury the nicked stem in the prepared drill and, using a split wooden clothes peg or wire clip, pin the stem securely in position. Water in well to encourage root growth and do not allow to dry out.

STAGE 1: Choose a low, level stem from an existing herb plant. Bend it down and make a slanting cut with a sharp knife in the under-side of the stem, about 20cm (8in) away from the main stem. Do not cut all the way through the stem. The purpose of the cut is to encourage new roots to form.

After four to six weeks, roots will have formed and you will have a whole new plant that can be severed from the parent plant.

Mound layering

This method is similar to layering. In spring, mound 7.5–12.5cm (3–5in) of a mixture of sand and peat over the crown of the plant so that only the young shoots at the top of the plant are exposed. This will encourage new shoots to develop roots. Replenish the sand/peat mixture if it is eroded by heavy rain, to keep the crown of the plant covered.

By late summer/autumn, roots will have formed and the shoots can be severed from the parent plant, dug up and replanted.

Plants suitable for mound layering

Cotton lavender (*Santolina chamaecyparissus*)
Hyssop (*Hyssopus officinalis*)
Rosemary (*Rosmarinus officinalis* 'Prostratus')
Sages (salvia)
Southernwood (*Artemisia abrotanum*)
Thymes (thymus)
Winter savory (*Satureja montana*)
Wormwood (*Artemisia absinthium*)

The leggy stems of sage, ready to layer

The finished mound layering around the sage

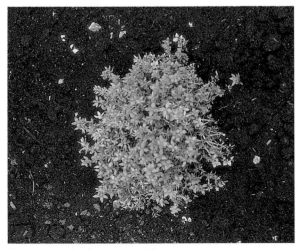

Thyme, ready for mound layering

Mound-layered thyme

ROOT DIVISION

Root division is probably the easiest way of increasing your herbs. It is a simple process which enables you to produce plants identical to the parent. Large clumps of herbaceous perennials can be pulled apart and small pieces replanted. Division is best done when the plants are dormant.

STAGE 1: Lift the whole clump with a fork and ease the soil from the roots, being careful not to damage them.

STAGE 2: Split the plant into sections by pulling it apart with your hands. Never use a spade as this is likely to damage the roots.

STAGE 3: After separating, make sure that the new, individual plants have strong growth buds and healthy roots.

STAGE 4: Plant as soon as possible, cutting back the top growth by one-half before planting.

Tough plants may be hard to pull apart. If so, use two forks to prise them apart. Place the forks in the centre of the plant, close together and placed back to back. Force the forks apart at the top, separating the plant at the bottom into at least two portions

Splitting a mint plant into sections by pulling it apart with the hands

Plants suitable for root division

Bergamot (*Monarda didyma*)

Catmint (*Nepeta cataria*)

Comfrey (*Symphytum officinale*)

Lady's mantle (*Alchemilla mollis*)

Lemon balm (*Melissa officinalis*)

Lovage (*Levisticum officinale*)

Marjorams (origanum)

Sweet cicely (*Myrrhis odorata*)

Violets (*Viola odorata*)

Plants with creeping roots

Mints (mentha)

Tansy (*Tanacetum vulgare*)

Herbs that grow from bulbs

Chives (*Allium schoenoprasum*)

Welsh onion (*Allium fistulosum*)

Herbs that will not grow from seed

Aloe (*Aloe vera*)

Tarragon (*Artemisia dracunculus*)

GROWING HERBS BOUGHT IN POTS

The quickest and easiest, although more expensive, way to establish your herb garden is to buy some of your plants from a garden centre or nursery. Always buy good quality plants, and try to select strong, healthy ones. If a plant looks straggly and wilting with yellowing leaves, leave it where it is. If, on the other hand, it has plenty of bushy, strong-looking growth with no discoloration, it is probably healthy.

Check stems, leaves and roots. Have a good look at the bottom of the pot. If the roots are pushing through the drainage holes, it has obviously outgrown its pot size, although there should be some root showing, as this is a sign of a well-developed, healthy root system. If you tap the side of the pot and the compost is loose, this is indicative of a specimen that hasn't had time to establish a strong root system. In either of these instances, it is inadvisable to buy.

Try to avoid buying herbs that are in flower; herbs transplant more easily before they bloom. Sometimes, growers over-force plants in greenhouses with the result that they are floppy and leggy. Occasionally, a grower will plant several small herbs in a pot to look like one bushy plant. These should be avoided. Try to resist the temptation of buying tender or half-hardy herbs before all risk of frost has passed, unless you have some means of protecting them.

Having selected your herbs and taken them home, place them in a warm, sheltered spot until you are ready to plant. Water them well if the compost is dry and plant them as soon as possible, either in early morning or in the evening. When planting, try not to disturb the rootball, and always dig a hole that is a little bigger than the pot itself.

Planting herbs grown in pots

STAGE 1: Make a planting hole.

STAGE 2: Hold the container in one hand and place your other hand over the top of the pot, with your fingers either side of the plant.

STAGE 3: Turn the container upside down, tapping the pot sharply on the sides. The plant will come away leaving the rootball intact.

STAGE 4: Using both hands, place the herb in the hole, making sure that the top of the compost around the plant is the same as the level of soil into which you are planting. If it is above this level, the plant will dry out.

STAGE 5: Fill in around with loose soil, press in gently and water well.

PLANTING INVASIVE HERBS

Invasive herbs such as the mints, tansy and woodruff need to have their spread restricted by planting them in sunken pots or buckets with their bottom removed. Heavy duty plastic bags can also be used, but be sure to make drainage holes.

STAGE 1: Dig a hole the same size and depth as your pot or bucket.

STAGE 2: Make sure that the pot's bottom has been removed and then place it, empty, in the hole, with its top level with the ground.

STAGE 3: Partially fill the container with compost. Plant the herb, adding more compost and firming in well. Continue to add compost until the rim of the container is covered. Water thoroughly.

STAGE 4: Each year, during spring, replant the herb and replace the compost in the container. The plant can be divided at this time, if necessary, and the young, vigorous pieces replanted in the same way.

PRUNING

Once herbs are established, the size and vigour of most of them can be controlled to some degree by harvesting and cutting back. While dormant plants may be tidied up during winter, the main time for pruning herbs is during spring and autumn.

Pruning produces vigorous new shoots from just below the pruning point, and it also allows light and air to reach all parts of the plant. Regular pruning needs to be carried out annually, and woody herbs, climbers and perennials all need some sort of trimming and pruning. Lightly trim herbs such as thyme directly after flowering so that the plant has time to make fresh growth before winter. At the end of the growing season, shrubby perennial herbs should be cut back to half the year's growth.

Woody trees and shrubs such as the evergreens box, bay and myrtle should be pruned in spring and again in autumn, if necessary, to maintain a sturdy, bushy shape. Deciduous herbs such as lemon verbena should be pruned in late winter or early spring when branches which have become too high or spreading need to be cut out, so that a compact, open shape is retained. Perennial herbs, such as fennel, mint, lady's mantle and tarragon, need to have all dead growth removed in winter.

Topiary

Many evergreen herbs – box, bay and myrtle, for example – can be trained into shaped forms and clipped according to design. The best way to do this is to plant cuttings with upright stems and then train the one stem to spiral up a central stake, which can later be removed. Box is a good subject for a spiral shape. Remember, though, that the plants will take time to achieve the desired height and shape. A topiary feature or geometric hedge needs two clippings each year, one in late spring and one in late summer.

Herbs suitable for potted topiary include cotton lavender (*Santolina chamaecyparissus*), myrtle (*Myrtus communis*) and rosemary (*Rosmarinus officinalis*).

An example of a clipped box bush

PESTS AND DISEASES

Generally speaking, well-grown, healthy herbs are relatively pest- and disease-free. They are also less vulnerable to attack because many of them contain aromatic oils which have insect repellent and anti-bacterial properties: for example, lavender, rosemary and thyme. Strong-smelling herbs, such as pennyroyal, tansy, cotton lavender, rue and curry plant, are also unlikely to fall victim, while chives and garlic too are remarkably resistant to infection.

Plants are much more susceptible to disease and pest infestation if they are weak and straggly and under stress, so the best defence against such attack is to grow them in a well-prepared soil with added compost and organic mulches and with the correct amount of nutrients and water. They also need spacious conditions where air and light can circulate – air circulation can be improved by planting at greater distances and pruning where appropriate. Always sow or plant your herbs at the best time of year so that they are well-established before there is any danger of pest infestation or disease.

Rubbish heaps, decaying crops and weeds can serve as hosts, as can dirty pots and seed trays, and soil brought into the greenhouse. Remove rotting leaves and debris and stick to a rigid hygiene regime.

Diseases

Most garden diseases are caused by fungi which are invisible to the naked eye and only recognized by the symptoms they cause.

Rusts

The fungi causing mint rust, for example, lie on the surface of the soil during winter. Probably the most effective treatment is to scatter dry straw over the mint in winter and set light to it. This will kill the spores in the soil, but will not harm the underground runners of the plant. Mint rust is easily recognizable by the orange-coloured spore pustules that appear on the leaves and stems which then become twisted and distorted. You can pick off and burn all the infected shoots to prevent the spores from being scattered, but the disease may eventually kill the plant. Alternatively, you can dig up and burn all the infected mint and replant new specimens in a different spot.

Chives can also be affected by a different type of rust, particularly in mild areas. Again, there is no cure, and if the plants are badly infected, they should be lifted and destroyed. Comfrey too is subject to rust attacks. Cut off the infected leaves and burn them.

Chive leaves, badly infected with rust

Downy mildew on borage

Rots and mildews

Garlic can be attacked by onion white rot, a fungal disease that rots the bulbs. The base of the bulb and the roots are smothered in a white, fluffy, fungal growth. All infected plants should be lifted and burned.

Powdery mildew is a common disease in sage, the mints and sometimes tarragon. Bergamot and sweet cicely can also suffer from powdery mildew, which thrives in dry, hot summers. It is recognizable by the greyish mould that appears on the leaves. A dusting of sulphur can act as a control measure when applied to the leaves. Tap watering may help.

Downy mildew, encouraged by cool, wet springs and autumns, can affect borage and evening primrose. The upper surface of the leaves becomes brown and blotched, while the underside has whitish patches.

Bay can suffer from scale: look for small, waxy scabs on the underside of the leaves and on the stems and rub them off with your hands.

Damping-off disease can affect seedlings and is caused by fungi that rot their base and stem. The fungi flourish in unhygienic, moist conditions. Once the disease is established, it cannot be controlled. Use a sterilized potting mixture, and water with a fungicidal solution when sowing and pricking out.

Pests

Prevention is better than cure. Inspect your herbs carefully, particularly during spring, when new growth is appearing, and in late summer when many insects lay eggs, and try to solve the problem before any damage occurs.

Aphids

Any plant that makes soft growth can be plagued by aphids which suck the sap from the leaves and shoots causing leaf curling and distortion, stunted growth and a sooty mould. These insects spread virus diseases from one plant to another, causing a considerable amount of damage. Aphids can be found on herbs such as poppies, anise, borage, angelica and the seed heads of fennel and dill.

Spray the affected plants with soapy water, or pinch out the affected tops. Lacewing larvae eat aphids, hoverflies and their larvae feed on them, as do ladybirds and their larvae. Ladybirds will also lay their eggs close to aphid colonies. Try to encourage insects such as these into your garden – grow nasturtiums, for example, which attract hoverflies – and if you must use an insecticide, use a selective, systemic insecticide, or an insecticidal soap, that leaves most beneficial garden insects unharmed.

Suckers

Bay and box can be attacked by suckers (psyllids); bay in the spring, box throughout the summer. Box leaves become stunted and the leaf margins of bay are thickened, curled and yellowed. The affected shoots should be cut out and burned.

Black aphids and a sooty mould on chamomile

Carrot fly

The larvae of the carrot fly (*Psila rosae*) affect parsley, causing it to develop discoloured foliage and even to eventually die. The fly lays eggs in the soil near the plant and the larvae hatch out and feed in the tissues of the larger roots, eating tunnels out of them. The older leaves then begin to yellow and droop, becoming tinged with red. A soil insecticide can be used or, alternatively, two batches of parsley can be raised each year, so that you have a replacement supply to plant on a different site.

Celery leaf miner

These larvae can disfigure the leaves of lovage, leaving a thin ribbon of dead tissue. The grub tunnels within the leaves, which should immediately be picked off and crushed.

Cuckoo spit

Cuckoo spit is caused by the larvae of the sap-sucker froghopper insect, and a large variety of plants are attacked in late spring by this insect, which sucks the sap and causes tender shoots to wilt and twist. Lavender shoots can become infested with frothy masses of cuckoo spit, as can southernwood and roses. The best way to deal with it is to pick it off by hand.

Red spider mite

A very persistent pest which flourishes in hot, dry conditions, such as those in a greenhouse. Eggs overwinter in cracks in the greenhouse and hatch in spring. Red spider mites feed on the plant's sap and attacks are evident by a fine webbing around the plant and a pale stippling of its leaves. Succulent-leaved herbs that are grown under glass are particularly vulnerable. Control the pests by keeping up humidity and by introducing the predatory mite *Phytoseiulus perimilis* to feed on them as temperatures increase. Re-introduce the predators as necessary.

Caterpillars

Caterpillars can be a nuisance from summer to early spring. These pests enjoy the young leaves of basil, sweet marjoram and summer savory. Pick them off by hand, or apply derris dust (see 'Using chemicals', page 59).

Slugs and snails

Slugs and snails can also cause havoc in the herb garden, although their damage can be limited by controlling their numbers. Slugs tend to attack the same herbs as caterpillars. Young bergamot shoots and parsley are also attractive to them. Slugs hide during the day and feed at night. Snails also hide during the day, usually in cool, moist, dark places.

A nocturnal hunt armed with a torch and a bucket of soapy water is one way of dealing with them. The skin of half a grapefruit or melon left on the ground also works: slugs and snails hide under it and can be removed the following morning. You could try sinking a small dish half-filled with milk or beer into the ground. Slugs love these and will fall in and drown. Keep the container about 2.5cm (1in) above ground level or beneficial ground beetles may also be drowned.

Snails are very fond of chamomile 'Treneague'

Particularly vulnerable plants can be surrounded by grit or crushed egg shells, and very small plants protected by covering them with a large plastic bottle with the bottom part cut off. Creating a shady canopy of herbs will prove advantageous for foraging ground beetles who have an enormous appetite for slugs.

Using chemicals

If you decide to use chemicals to rid yourself of pests and diseases, certain precautions must be taken. Many herbs are edible, so it is vital to make sure that the product you have chosen is suitable. Always read the instructions on the packet and try to keep the use of chemicals to a minimum.

In small gardens, pests can often be washed away with a hose pipe.

Derris dust, an organic product, will destroy aphids and caterpillars, for example, although, on the minus side, it will also destroy beneficial insects, such as ladybirds and butterflies, and is somewhat toxic as well. If you do use it, be sure not to pick your herbs for at least two weeks after applying, and to wash them well before using.

COMPANION PLANTING

Companion planting works due to the scents of certain plants acting as deterrents to insect and other garden pests, and many herbs make excellent companion plants to other plants in your garden.

Grow basil near tomatoes to deter whitefly, and feverfew with carrots to help keep carrot fly away. Plant garlic around the base of peach trees to help control the spread of peach leaf curl and with roses to produce a stronger perfume. Marigolds can help keep tomatoes pest-free, and a row of summer savory surrounding the broad bean patch will deter blackfly. Chamomile, known as the 'plants' physician', can aid any sickly plant.

Fragrant herbs are generally useful in maintaining a healthy vegetable patch. Try growing hyssop near cabbages to deter cabbage white butterflies, spearmint near roses to repel aphids, and tansy near fruit trees to repel insects. Rosemary planted in the rose garden is reputed to keep the roses healthy. A clump of Solomon's seal planted with lily of the valley is said to increase the size of the flowers and to keep the bed healthy.

Plant feverfew with carrots to help keep carrot fly away from the vegetables

4 GROWING HERBS IN CONTAINERS AND RAISED BEDS

CHOOSING CONTAINERS

Nowadays it is possible to buy containers of all shapes and sizes and in a variety of materials ranging from terracotta to plastic. And, choosing which ones to buy is, without doubt, one of the most exciting aspects of container gardening.

Go to any garden centre or nursery and you will discover a bewildering range of troughs, tubs and pots. Container sizes, shapes and designs must be carefully considered when you are planning your garden, and chosen with an eye to suiting both the style of your house and your garden. Ideally, they should be an integral part of the garden, having a definite purpose and a specific role to play, whether as a focal point, or to create interest, texture and colour.

Well-thought-out and well-planted containers give immediate impact. They can

A selection of basils, planted together, using a large plastic pot and various smaller ones

be used to fill gaps in borders, to stand on each side of a doorway, or as focal points to draw the eye to various parts of the garden, their simple lines providing structure and form. They also create an instant garden and a dramatic display that is both flexible and movable. Big, bold, classic containers can be used to create mood and atmosphere, and to give a range of stunning effects. Large terracotta pots make a statement all of their own, while plain, clay pots are a very good choice for architectural plants.

Plastic pots

Your choice of pots will depend largely on your budget. Plastic pots are reasonably cheap to buy. They are lightweight, easy to store and clean, and they will not crack once the nights become frosty. It is also possible to judge their water content merely by lifting them. Cheap polythene pots are ideal for annual herb displays, as most of the pot will be hidden from view. Remember, though, to gouge out drainage holes before planting. Another choice might be mock terracotta pots moulded from polypropylene, which give the appearance of terracotta and provide insulation for the compost.

Clay and terracotta pots

Clay and terracotta pots are more expensive, with the plain, machine-made ones being the cheapest. Again, the cheaper ones are ideal when the main focus of attention is upon the display of herbs. Clay pots dry out more quickly than plastic ones, so they will need to be watered more frequently, or lined with polythene – or you could use a soil-based compost. Clay and terracotta pots are heavy to move around, however, and if the compost inside freezes during winter, they may crack. You can insulate the outside by tying bubble

A large, plastic herb pot, six weeks after planting

wrap around them. Remember to soak new pots in water for 24 hours before using.

Glazed earthenware pots

Glazed earthenware pots give you a great choice of colour and design, and the glazing prevents water loss. Not all glazed pots have drainage holes, however, so check this before buying. Again, these pots may crack if the compost freezes.

Pot marigold will add vibrant colour to any pot

Concrete pots

Concrete pots can be bought in a variety of designs and mouldings. They are extremely stable and frost-resistant, but are heavy to move around. They can take a long time to become 'weathered', making them rather bleak in appearance. Use them for housing permanent hardy herbs.

Reconstituted stone pots

These are manufactured from stone which is ground up and then moulded into shape. They take a while to 'weather' and are heavy to move around, but they are both frost-resistant and stable.

Wooden half barrels

Wooden half barrels make stunning containers for herb displays, and they are stable and frost resistant. Some half barrels, however, are replicas, and may have plywood bases and inferior metal bands, making their lifespan a short one. They may also fall apart if allowed to dry out, and you will probably need to drill drainage holes before planting.

Fibreglass containers

These are expensive, but modern and stylish. They have a high gloss finish, and come in a variety of colours, but can crack or shatter if knocked. They are more stable than plastic pots, frost-resistant, and relatively easy to move around.

SUITABLE CONTAINER HERBS

There are a variety of herbs that grow well in containers, but always bear in mind that the herbs you choose will have to live and grow in pots, which means regular watering, although big containers and containers grouped together need less watering. If you group your pots, for the best appearance do so in odd rather than even numbers and in small groups, and don't mix those made from different materials.

Nasturtiums with their cheerful colour and holy basil will grow happily together in a pot

Herbs to try in containers or pots

Basil (*Ocimum basilicum*) loves the sun so can be potted and grown in full sunshine

Fennel (*Foeniculum vulgare*) can be grown in a container and kept small by pinching out its growing points

Golden marjoram (*Origanum vulgare* 'Aureum') should be planted in a 20–30cm (8–12in) pot

Lemon verbena (*Aloysia triphylla*) thrives in a pot

Myrtle (*Myrtus communis*) should be planted in a 20–30cm (8–12in) pot

Nasturtium (*Tropaeolum majus* 'Alaska') is a neat and bushy plant very suitable for container growing

Parsley (*Petroselinum crispum*)

Pot marigolds (*Calendula officinalis*) add vibrant colour

Rock hyssop (*Hyssopus officinalis* subsp. *aristatus*) is aromatic, neat and compact

Sages (salvia), with their various leaf colourings, are also a good basis for any collection of containers

Salad burnet (*Sanguisorba minor*) can be grown in a pot, as can

Scented-leaf geraniums (pelargonium)

Sweet marjoram (*Origanum majorana*)

Thymes (thymus) are small and drought resistant. Try growing them individually in pots or in combinations with other herbs.

Invasive herbs invade neighbouring plants and are best grown in a pot

Creeping Jenny (*Lysimachia nummularia* 'Aurea') grows well in a container, tending to hang down the sides

Horseradish (*Armoracia rusticana*)

Lemon balm (*Melissa officinalis*)

Mints (mentha)

Tarragon (*Artemisia dracunculus*)

Suitable for tubs

Bay (*Laurus nobilis*)

English lavender (*Lavandula angustifolia*)

Rosemary (*Rosmarinus officinalis*)

Herbs for small troughs

Basil (*Ocimum basilicum* 'Mini Purpurascens Wellsweep')

Lemon thyme (*Thymus* x *citriodorus*)

Parsley (*Petroselinum crispum*)

Creeping Jenny will hang vertically down the sides when planted in a container

Red basil adds a splash of colour to any type of container planting

GROUPING HERBS

Having decided what to plant, try to co-ordinate herbs of a similar colour to your initial choice, so that the same colour scheme predominates. Don't be deterred if you think a combination won't work. Experiment, remembering to avoid combining opposing extremes: for instance, don't plant sun-loving herbs with those that prefer damp, shady conditions. And, if a selection of herbs is planted together, make sure that they all grow at roughly the same rate.

Planting distances will be shown on seed packets or on plant labels if the herbs are bought from a garden centre or nursery, but it is not necessary to adhere to these when planting up pots. You can use relatively small plants and move them out when they get too big, as you would with any potted plants. You can then fill the spaces that are left with smaller specimens of the same herb.

Hyssop, rue and sage, planted together

If you want to create a calm, relaxed effect, go for large dramatic containers and plant herbs with strong structural foliage for real impact. One large container can look stunning if positioned correctly.

Alternatively, herbs can be planted in separate, smaller pots which can then be built up in attractive groups of different colour schemes. Isolated colour ranges draw the eye and attract attention. Containers spilling over with a single herb variety can give maximum impact.

A planting of marjoram, sage, mint, thyme, parsley and chives in a half barrel

Box, violets, thyme, heartsease and nasturtiums

Feverfew, sweet basil and golden marjoram

Golden oregano and chamomile

Herb combinations

- *Thymus vulgaris* 'Silver Posie' with chives and purple-leaved sage.
- A combination of golden marjoram, dill, tansy, feverfew and marigold.
- Cotton lavender, clary sage, borage, blue rue and pinks combine well.
- Mix sage, chives, marjoram and thyme (sage and thyme are evergreens, the others are perennials). Add a few annual herbs such as basil.
- Rosemary, winter savory, sage, thyme and marjoram can either be grown in one large pot or in separate pots.
- Plant chervil, coriander and parsley and place in a bright position out of the sun.
- Chives, variegated mint, purple-leaved sage, marjoram, thyme and parsley make a lovely combination (see page 64, lower left).
- Try mixing bay, oregano, golden curled marjoram, bush or Greek basil (*Ocimum basilicum* var. *minimum*) and golden thyme.
- Decorative plants such as rue, rosemary, lemon balm and marigold look well grouped together.
- Parsley, chives, basil, thyme (*Thymus vulgaris* 'Silver Queen'), golden marjoram (curled) (*Origanum vulgare* 'Aureum Crispum').

- Mix bronze fennel (*Foeniculum vulgare* 'Purpureum'), wild celery (*Apium graveolens*), variegated lemon balm (*Melissa officinalis* 'Aurea'), thyme 'Silver Posie', double chamomile (*Chamaemelum nobile* 'Flore Pleno'), heartsease, camphor thyme (*Thymus mastichina*) and curry plant.
- Try a low terracotta bowl containing small, clipped box and low thymes.
- *Lavandula angustifolia* 'Hidcote', pineapple sage (*Salvia elegans* 'Scarlet PIneapple') and scented-leaf geranium.
- Thyme 'Silver Posie', chives and purple-leaved sage (*Salvia officinalis* 'Purpurascens').
- Golden marjoram (*Origanum vulgare* 'Aureum'), golden thyme (*Thymus citriodorus* 'Aureus'), golden sage (*Salvia officinalis* var. *Icterina*) and tricolour sage (*Salvia officinalis* var. *tricolor*) in 20–30cm (8–12in) pots.
- Hyssop, rue and sage all go well together, but need pruning to keep top growth under control (see page 64, top).
- Chamomile, scented-leaf geranium, golden marjoram, oregano, sage, parsley and thyme.
- Clipped bay, sage, thyme, chives and mint make an attractive group.

PLANTING POTS, TUBS AND TROUGHS

Always set tubs or troughs in their final positions before filling and planting. When planting tubs and troughs, use a loam-based compost – it provides body and the anchorage that herbs need – with one-third as much of grit mixed into it.

Planting a variety of herbs in a large pot

Materials for planting a large herb pot

Make sure that the drainage is good by placing a deep layer of hardcore – it also adds weight and stability – at the bottom. Place large pieces over the drainage holes and then a layer of smaller pieces on top to a depth of at least 2.5cm (1in). Add some peat or pulverized bark on top of the hardcore to prevent the compost from washing away.

You can line the containers with plastic sheeting to help conserve water, or sink an upturned, bottomless, plastic bottle into the compost to allow water to penetrate the roots of the plants. Place a layer of compost over the peat or bark.

An hour or so before planting, stand each herb in its container in a bucket of water, almost up to its rim, so that the rootball has a thorough soaking.

Before planting the herbs, place them, still in their pots, in the tub or trough and move them around until you get a balanced effect. An informal planting is better than a regimented look. Walk around the container and view it from all angles. Place tall plants at the back or sides and shorter or trailing ones at the front, or sometimes at the sides if the planting calls for it. If the container is to be viewed from all sides, arrange the herbs so that the tallest ones are in the centre and grade them down towards the sides. Plant so that the tub looks reasonably full, but allow room for the plants to spread during summer. Summer containers can be planted as early as late spring if they can be kept frost-free.

After planting, cover the surface of the compost with a topping of small pebbles to act as a mulch – to prevent water from evaporating too quickly – and to give the container a neat finish. Give it a good watering – this will help settle the compost – using a fine rose, watering the foliage as well to remove any soil particles. Water when the container is in shade as the rays of the sun on the wet leaves could damage them.

PLANTING WINDOW BOXES

Window boxes are available in various materials, including terracotta, plastic and wood. Always check that the fixing used on your window box is strong and secure enough to take its weight when full. Check also that you are legally entitled to have a window box.

If you prefer to make your own window box, choose treated hardwood, such as elm, beech or oak. The finished box should have drainage holes, be treated with preservative and lined with polythene sheeting. Use a loam-based compost and add water-retaining polymer granules. These absorb large amounts of moisture which is then released over a long period of time. Alternatively, herbs can be potted up individually, so that any that fail can be replaced easily. The smaller perennial herbs, such as chives,

marjoram, the thymes, winter savory, salad burnet, scented-leaf geraniums, pineapple mint and parsley are the most suitable.

STAGE 1: Place a layer of crocks over the drainage holes in the base of the window box.

STAGE 2: Mix loam-based compost and a little sharp sand together and fill the box to within 2.5cm (1in) of the top.

STAGE 3: Dig planting holes in the mixture to the depth of each herb in its pot. Loosen the rootballs by gently tapping the sides of the pot on a hard surface, and place the herbs in the planting holes.

STAGE 4: Move the compost around the plants and firm in. Water well.

A decorative window box filled with a combination of herbs

PLANTING HANGING BASKETS

Hanging baskets are the perfect way to add height to any planting scheme and, whilst they are possibly the smallest garden feature, they are the ones that provide immediate impact.

First, you need to consider the type and size of basket you prefer: plastic coated wire, those made of plastic, or even clay pots held in rope nets. A popular choice is the round-bottomed, wire basket that can be lined with a variety of materials, from the traditional sphagnum moss to preformed wood fibre liners. Wool 'moss' liner is an ideal substitute for natural moss and is suitable for any shaped basket, as well as having excellent water-retaining properties.

STAGE 1: Line your basket with moss or a bought liner.

STAGE 2: Place a disc of polythene in the bottom of the basket to help retain moisture. Add a little multi-purpose compost and mix in some water-retaining granules. If your basket insists on moving, stand it in a bucket or large pot.

A herb hanging basket, two months after planting

STAGE 3: Plant the outside of the basket first, working from the bottom up.

STAGE 4: Gently open up any slits in the outside of the lining, or make your own planting holes, and insert one plant into each slit/hole from the inside, if possible, trying not to damage the rootball.

STAGE 5: Fill with compost as you go along, firming it around each plant.

STAGE 6: Build up in layers, finally planting the top of the basket.

STAGE 7: Water the basket well and stand it in a frost-free place to settle. Follow up with a daily watering.

Materials for planting a hanging basket: select those that will complement the rest of the garden

Take care to water the finished basket evenly. Supplementary feeding will be needed in six weeks

MAKING A SINK GARDEN

Raised sink gardens make an attractive, miniature herb garden for both the patio and the terrace. Restricted to plants with similar requirements and placed in an open, sunny situation, they can be an eye-catching feature. Nowadays, however, old stone sinks are both expensive and difficult to find, but glazed sinks, when coated in hypertufa (a mixture of peat substitute, cement, grit or sand and water) make excellent substitutes. They also have several advantages: the plug hole ensures adequate drainage, exactly the right mixture of soil can be used, and the plants themselves can receive greater individual attention which will help them to thrive.

A hypertufa-covered sink planted with herbs

COVERING A GLAZED SINK

You will need:
Tile cutter
Adhesive, eg Unibond
Paintbrush
Old bucket
Trowel
1–2 parts peat substitute, sieved
1 part cement
2 parts fine grit or coarse sand
Heavy-duty gloves

STAGE 1: Make sure the sink is clean, dry and free from grease.

STAGE 2: Score the surfaces to be coated with a tile cutter, to give a rough surface for the hypertufa to adhere to.

STAGE 5: When the bonding agent becomes tacky, apply the hypertufa mix. The covering should be about 1.5–2cm (½–¾in) thick.

STAGE 3: Mix together the peat substitute, cement and fine grit or coarse sand and add sufficient water to form a thick paste.

STAGE 6: Before the mixture sets, roughen the surface with a stiff brush so that it resembles the texture of stone.

STAGE 4: Using a paintbrush, cover the surfaces with adhesive. Paint both the outside and 10cm (4in) of the inside, to reach below the final compost level, so the hypertufa adheres well.

STAGE 7: It will take about a week for the hypertufa to dry, after which time the surface should be scrubbed with a brush and then washed down well.

Siting a sink garden

The sink should be raised off the ground, about 45cm (18in) – or 75cm (30in) for wheelchair users – on supports of brick columns at each corner. This will improve the drainage, provide a good setting for the sink, and will also give a better view of the herbs. Any supports should be stable enough to bear the weight of the sink when filled, so that there is no danger of it tipping, and they should always be placed on a level area rather than a sloping one. Make sure that the drainage hole isn't blocked by the supports and that the sink is placed in an open position that will provide both an adequate amount of sun and shelter from the wind.

Planting a sink garden

Cover the base with a layer of rubble and then fill one quarter of the sink with gravel. Place a layer of inverted, thinly cut turf over the gravel, and then fill the remainder with a mixture of sand and compost. To add interest, position a few rocks in the sink as it is filled, bedding them in well to at least one-third of their depth.

Planting the first herb in the sink garden

Choose your herbs carefully. Compact species are ideal as the more vigorous kinds can overrun the weaker ones and quickly deplete available nutrients. Draw a plan of your planting scheme on paper, labelling each herb and noting its height and spread. Keeping to your plan, dig the required number of planting holes and place your plants in them. Fill in around each plant with compost, firm, and water thoroughly. Add a layer of gravel as a top-dressing.

A sink garden will need to be replanted from time to time when the nutrients are exhausted. Carefully remove the plants and trim their roots and top-growth. Replace the old compost with new, reposition the herbs and add a top-dressing of gravel.

Burying rocks to one-third of their depth

Sink garden planting suggestions

Bush basil (*Ocimum basilicum* var. *minimum*)
Compact marjoram (*Origanum vulgare* 'Compactum')
Nasturtium (*Tropaeolum majus* 'Alaska')
Pinks (dianthus)
Rock hyssop (*Hyssopus officinalis* subsp. *aristatus*)
Thymes (thymus)

PLANTING A STRAWBERRY POT

A strawberry pot planted with herbs is a very attractive feature, but bear in mind the height and spread of the herbs before planting. Use a frost-resistant planter with good drainage and good-sized planting holes.

STAGE 1: Place hardcore in the bottom of the container and add a good layer of multi-purpose compost up to the bottom of the lowest holes.

STAGE 2: Starting from the bottom, insert the herbs into the side pockets. Fill with compost as you go, making sure that there is room for the rootball only, with no empty spaces that would make air pockets.

STAGE 3: Continue in this way until the top is reached. Complete the pot with the crown planting. Water the pot well.

STAGE 4: Keep the compost moist and feed once a week from spring (when you plant it) to late summer.

Strawberry pot planting suggestions
Side plantings
Thymes
    (*Thymus* 'Hartington Silver')
    (*Thymus vulgaris* 'Silver Posie')
    2 x (*Thymus serpyllum* 'Snowdrift')
    2 x Lemon thyme (*Thymus* x *citriodorus*)
    (*Thymus azoricus*)
    (*Thymus serpyllum* 'Goldstream')
    Orange-scented thyme (*Thymus*
        fragrantissimus)
Creeping savory (*Satureja spicigera*)
Compact marjoram (*Origanum vulgare*
    'Compactum')

Crown planting
Golden marjoram, curled (*Origanum vulgare*
    'Aureum Crispum')
Hyssop (*Hyssopus officinalis*)
Painted sage (*Salvia viridis*)
Sweet basil (*Ocimum basilicum*)

A strawberry pot, two months after planting

PATIOS, BALCONIES AND ROOF GARDENS

Patios

Patios are one of the most popular places for containers, where they can be grouped for maximum impact and to add vibrance and colour, enhancing the overall effect. Try containers of contrasting shape, adding plants to suit that shape: trailing herbs in tall pots, for example.

Give some thought to foliage colours. Red and green and red and yellow foliage are good combinations and can be planted in individual pots and arranged together in groups. If the patio is paved with slabs, an occasional slab can be lifted and herbs planted in the exposed soil. Try to create a linking theme between containers, such as a number of varieties or colours of the same herb, to add interest and impact.

Balconies and roof gardens

First, make sure that your roof will support the materials needed for the garden, or a variety of pots. Invest in a structural survey to ascertain the maximum weight your roof will take. Remember the legalities. Do you need planning permission? What about building regulations? Cost should also be taken into account. You will need timber, compost, pots and plants – the kind and amount will depend upon what you decide to do – but the cost could well run into triple figures.

And yet, what could be more delightful than your very own roof garden, fragrant with herbs such as tangy lemon verbena and aromatic rosemary, with jasmine, roses and

An array of herb pots on a patio provides interest throughout the growing season

A group of herbs on a balcony aids privacy

honeysuckle growing in profusion? The weather can, of course, be more extreme on roofs and balconies, although the impact of the wind can be lessened by a careful choice and placing of trellis and fencing. Choose pots made from fibreglass or other lightweight substances, and use lightweight drainage material such as polystyrene, rather than crocks. These containers will need careful anchoring, so top the compost with gravel to hold it down.

A roof garden can be formal or informal. Try growing *Buddleia globosa* with its orange balls of flowers to attract butterflies, and evergreens such as box for winter interest. Remember to arrange some of your containers to create shaded areas where shade-loving herbs such as pennyroyal, mint, valerian and woodruff can be planted.

CONTAINER MAINTENANCE

Check and water your containers even after rain, because the 'umbrella' of leaves prevents the rain from reaching the compost, making the plants begin to wilt fairly quickly. Never allow your tubs and troughs to dry out or to become waterlogged, and always keep a full can of water to hand so that the water you use is at the same temperature as the atmosphere. Dead head flowers regularly to prevent self-seeding, and remove decaying foliage and any dead leaves or wood on a regular basis. Apply a liquid feed once a fortnight during summer.

Regular watering is essential for potted herbs

A raised bed, made from log slices, approximately two months after planting

RAISED BEDS

If the soil in your garden is heavy clay or poorly drained, try growing your herbs in raised beds. They can be any shape you choose and can be constructed from bricks, natural stone, hardwood railway sleepers and sections of trees. They are ideal for disabled gardeners, who can garden without bending or from a wheelchair. Blind gardeners will also have the pleasure of scents and textures within easy reach and at a manageable height.

Make sure your raised bed is of a practical size – the best height being between 30cm–1m (12–39in), although 75cm (30in) would be an ideal height for wheelchair users.

Raised beds ensure the drainage that most herbs need, and the soil, because it is raised, warms up more quickly in spring, allowing annual herbs to be sown earlier in the year. Try to make sure that the bed receives some sunshine during the day and that it is of a

size which allows you to reach your herbs easily. Raised beds tend to dry out quickly, so frequent watering will be necessary during hot, dry weather.

Making a raised bed from log slices

You will need:
Log slices, coated with preservative – those wired together are ideal. The height of the log slices should be that of the finished bed plus 2.5–5cm (1–2in).
Rubble
Compost
Waterproof material (optional, depending on site of bed)
4 x wire spikes for corners
Ball of string
Short wooden stakes or pegs
Wooden mallet

STAGE 1: Select the site and measure out the width, depth and height of the bed. Clear the area, and mark the size with stakes/pegs and string.

STAGE 2: Dig a shallow trench, 2.5–5cm (1–2in) deep, all the way round in which to place the ends of the log slices.

STAGE 3: Lay the logs along the trench to the length required. Wired log slices come in 1.2m (4ft) lengths (approx). If necessary, join each length together with the wire supplied.

STAGE 4: Drive a substantial spike into the ground at each corner of the bed. Attach the logs to the spike for support.

STAGE 5: If erecting a free-standing bed, complete the rectangle with logs. If backing the raised bed on to an existing feature, such as a wall, then you will only need a front and two sides. If building against a wall, then the wall will need to be protected with waterproof material before the bed is filled.

STAGE 6: Tap the logs into place with a wooden mallet to ensure a level finish, and tramp the soil firmly with your feet for support at the base.

Planting a raised bed

You will need:
Rubble
Rough peat or leaf mould
Compost
Selection of herbs

STAGE 1: After construction, place a 7.5–10cm (3–4in) layer of hardcore in the bottom of the bed to act as a drainage layer.

STAGE 2: Top with a layer of rough peat or leaf mould.

STAGE 3: Finish by filling with a multi-purpose compost.

STAGE 4: Plant the herbs, having first planned the plantings on paper. Water in well, and water frequently in hot weather.

5 GROWING AND USING CULINARY HERBS

Growing and using culinary herbs can be extremely satisfying. They can transform everyday dishes, stimulate the appetite and aid a balanced diet. They are added as flavourings to enhance simple dishes, as well as giving a touch of luxury to more adventurous and exotic ones. In fact, they help to improve almost all foods.

Culinary herbs have highly flavoured leaves, stems, flowers or seeds and benefit from regular harvesting which helps to keep them pest free and encourages strong, healthy growth. Most species are hardy. Grow them as near to the kitchen as possible for ease of access in all weathers, or site pots of the herbs you use most near the kitchen door.

A selection of culinary herbs grown in a trough gives a ready supply of herbs near a kitchen door

CHOOSING HERBS

When choosing herbs, start with a small selection that you know you are likely to use. You can then build upon this foundation, adding to it, and experimenting with different flavours as you go along. The most used culinary herbs are basil, bay, chives, marjoram, mint, parsley, rosemary, sage, tarragon and thyme. This selection will probably provide you with all your immediate needs.

When selecting your herbs, basic perennials are always a good choice: mint, fennel, tarragon, thyme and chives, for example. Other perennials to try are lovage, rosemary, sage and winter savory. You might also add the biennials parsley, caraway and garlic – although garlic and parsley are treated as annuals – and the annuals sweet marjoram and basil. Other annuals that could be included are chervil, summer savory and coriander. You could also grow several species of basil, thyme, marjoram and mint, all of which would give you a greater range of flavours from which to choose.

Sweet basil, feverfew and marjoram

If you like fish, try growing dill, mint, fennel and sorrel (*Rumex acetosa*). Salad lovers might care to plant rocket, chervil, salad burnet, sorrel and purslane (*Portulaca oleracea*), while meat eaters might like to grow rosemary, thyme and juniper (*Juniperus communis*). Borage could also be included, but the leaves, which are succulent and cooling, should be eaten when young and tender as they become quite bristly with age.

In early summer, the herbs will need a trim to keep their foliage leafy and fresh. Rosemary and thyme should be pruned in spring, with the soft tips removed throughout the summer. Give chives a trim in early summer to produce a second flush of young leaves that will last through the rest of the summer. Do not allow your culinary herbs to flower if you want them to keep on growing and producing lots of fresh leaves for the pot. The leaves of plants that are allowed to flower will be of poor quality, and the plants themselves will become leggy and sparse. Pick any new shoots to encourage plant growth.

Chives in flower

DESIGNING A SMALL CULINARY HERB GARDEN

There are various ways of planning such a garden. Access is an important consideration when siting any herb garden. A square plot in a cruciform design, for example, will give four square beds separated by brick, stone or crazy-paving paths. A focal point such as a potted bay, a bird bath or a sundial can then be placed at the intersections. Space will obviously dictate the size of the garden and be the limiting factor regarding the number and kinds of herbs you can grow. Some of the larger herbs may have to be omitted. If space is a real problem, however, the sides of gravel paths and rockeries are ideal for growing herbs such as thyme, marjoram, tarragon, rosemary and savory.

Another idea is a chessboard design (see page 14). Each herb would then be kept within its own boundaries, and the design could be edged with parsley, or even with bushy thyme. If space permitted, another type of formal garden could be laid out with a focal point in the centre and paths of gravel running between the beds of herbs. It could take the form of a square or rectangle and be enclosed by a hedge of rosemary or lavender. Edgings for the individual beds could be of chervil, curled parsley, lemon thyme, bush basil (*Ocimum basilicum* var. *minimum*) or hyssop. A cartwheel (see page 16) is a traditional favourite for plantings of culinary herbs, or try planting a selection of them in a herb ladder (see page 19). Sorrel, chervil and tarragon would be good subjects for this.

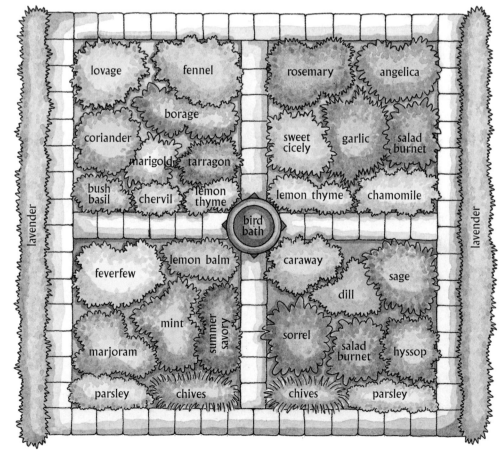

A plan of a cruciform culinary herb garden

Rocket grown in an informal setting

Why not plant an informal culinary herb garden with a variety of herbs arranged randomly together according to size, habit and planting needs, and with stepping stones in between them for ease of maintenance and harvesting? Try chervil, thyme, chives, sweet basil, tarragon, mint, rosemary, dill, summer savory, marjoram and parsley. The whole garden could then be surrounded by a hedge of lavender, rosemary or hyssop.

Alternatively, your culinary herb garden could take the form of a corner plot, backed on two sides by a wall or fence. Taller herbs, such as angelica, fennel and lovage could be grouped towards the back, with herbs such as lemon balm, sage, tarragon, salad burnet and borage to the front of them. Parsley, thyme and chives could provide a front border.

SITING CULINARY HERBS IN THE VEGETABLE PLOT

The traditional vegetable plot is usually situated in a sunny, sheltered position and provides an excellent place for growing herbs. Ideally, it should face south so that it receives plenty of sun, and be as close to the house as possible, with a path leading to and around it for easy access. Its size and design will be dictated by the type and amount of vegetables and herbs you wish to grow.

Should your vegetable plot be sited in a shady spot, choose herbs that will tolerate shade: mint, parsley, chervil, marjoram and sorrel, for example. You could also try companion planting, selecting those herbs suited to the well-being of the vegetables: sweet basil, for instance, is often grown with tomatoes to deter whitefly.

Lemon mint has attractive foliage as well as a delightful scent

Potagers

The French idea of a potager, where herbs, vegetables and fruit are grown together, is another idea. If space is limited, a potager 3–4m (10–13ft) will produce a reasonable range and quantity of produce. The vegetables and fruit could be interspersed with herbs such as sorrel, mint, chervil and chives and there could be a central focal point of lavender and marigolds planted in a large tub.

To make it look more attractive, it could be enclosed in low, wooden border sections, inside which an edging of various thymes – lemon and common thyme, for example – could be planted.

Lavender and marigolds, in a container, make an attractive combination as a centrepiece

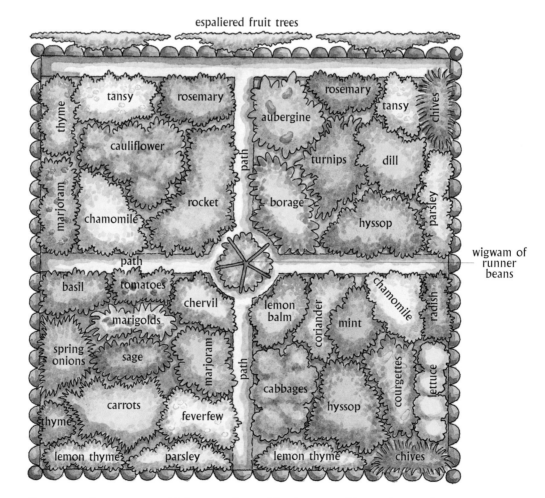

A plan of a neatly arranged potager, combining a variety of herbs, vegetables and some fruit trees

If you prefer to grow more herbs than vegetables, then you should consider replacing vegetable crops with herbs such as marjoram, sage, thyme, parsley, rosemary, and lemon balm. Plant perennial herbs such as marjoram, thyme and chives near the edges of the potager so that they are handy for harvesting. Annual and biennial herbs such as chervil, dill, borage, coriander and rocket (*Eruca vesicaria* subsp. *sativa*) can be planted in convenient gaps, but remember that these gaps will exist again once the herbs are removed at the end of the growing season.

In order to produce succulent crops, your potager will need fertile soil, rich in organic matter. So, if you are starting from scratch, you will need to dig the plot, incorporating plenty of rich compost as you go along, especially to soils that are heavy to start with. Remember not to overcrowd your potager, and try not to sow seed in rows, better to broadcast it over its own particular section. Lettuce and radish, for example, can be sown a little at a time, and the exercise repeated every few weeks. Keep the soil fertile, but do not overfeed.

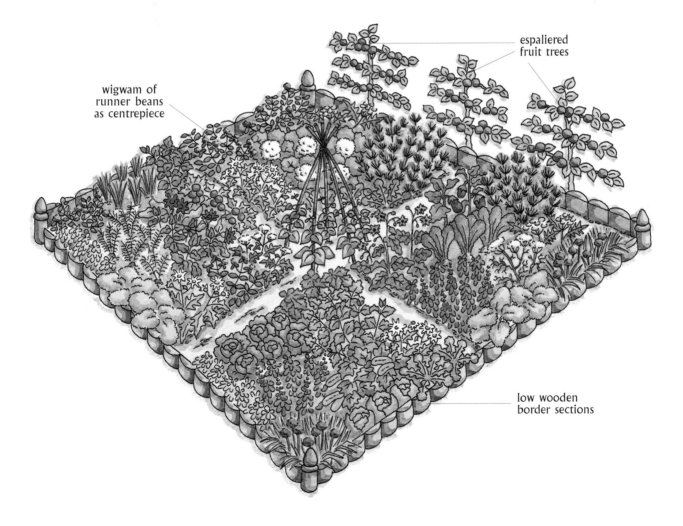

espaliered fruit trees

wigwam of runner beans as centrepiece

low wooden border sections

A three-dimensional view of a potager, showing a border of split logs and bisected by paths for easy access

POPULAR CULINARY HERBS

All culinary herbs are relatively simple to grow. As a beginner, it makes sense to buy a few perennial herbs such as bay, rosemary and sage to get you started. The selection of plants at specialist herb nurseries is much wider than at your local garden centre, so they are worth a visit. You can grow some perennials from seed, but bear in mind that if you do, you will not be able to harvest the plants until they are fully grown.

Ten of the best culinary herbs
Sweet basil

A delicate, half-hardy annual growing 45cm (18in) high, sweet basil (*Ocimum basilicum*) has light green leaves and produces creamy-white flowers in small spikes in summer. It has a mild aniseed, clove-like flavour, likes the sun, and flourishes in a rich, light, well-drained soil.

Seed should be sown in a seed tray at a temperature above 13°C (55°F) in mid- to late spring under cover. Keep watering to a minimum after germination. When large enough to handle, prick out the seedlings into individual pots filled with a free-draining compost.

Don't plant them outside until all risk of frost has passed. When planting, space the plants about 23–30cm (9–12in) apart.

Seed can also be sown during early to mid-summer and the plants brought indoors in early autumn.

Pinch out the growing tips when the plants have made growth of around 30–45cm (12–18in). This will prevent them from flowering and produce bushier plants.

When harvesting, pick the leaves from the top of the plant. The bottom pair of leaves die off continually, so, when picking, make sure that there are at least two pairs of leaves

A selection of basils can be grown together and placed near the kitchen door

left on the plant. Keep watering to a minimum and water in the morning – the herb hates wet roots at night.

Bush basil (*Ocimum basilicum* var. *minimum*), known also as Greek basil, is a compact variety, reaching a height of only 15–30cm (6–12in), making it ideal for container growing.

Other varieties include cinnamon basil (*Ocimum basilicum* 'Cinnamon'), with its spicy, slightly cinnamon flavour, 'Dark Opal' basil (*Ocimum basilicum* var. *aurauascens* 'Dark Opal') with its dark, purple-black leaves, the frilly lettuce-leaf basil (*Ocimum basilicum* var. *lactucafolium*), with its sweet tasting leaves, or 'Purple Ruffles' (*Ocimum basilicum* var. *aurauascens* 'Purple Ruffles'), another ornamental variety that is extremely tasty.

Sweet or knotted marjoram

Several marjorams are generally available, but three are important in the area of cooking: sweet or knotted marjoram (*Origanum majorana*), pot marjoram (*Origanum onites*) and wild marjoram (*Origanum vulgare*).

Sweet marjoram, a tender perennial usually treated as a half-hardy annual in temperate climates, is fairly mild and safe to use in quantity. It grows to around 30cm (12in) in height and has small, greyish green leaves which have an unusual sweet taste and are slightly hairy. Small, round heads, like knots, of creamy flowers appear in mid- to late summer. Sweet marjoram dislikes the cold.

Seed should be sown in trays in mid-spring and seedlings planted out in late spring at a spacing of 15cm (6in) apart. Seed can also be sown outside in late spring in a fertile, well-drained, medium soil and a sunny position. The seedlings grow slowly and good weeding is very important.

Pot marjoram, a perennial herb, can be grown for winter use, even though it is less well flavoured than sweet marjoram. The plant grows to a height of 60cm (24in), and has small leaves, hairy stems and pink or white flowers.

Wild marjoram is also known as oregano and is the easiest of the marjorams to grow. It benefits from lime and needs a well-drained soil and sunshine. Wild marjoram, which has a good, strong flavour, dies back in autumn, and its roots should be protected from the cold during winter with a light covering of leaf mould.

Pot and wild marjorams depend less on warmth than sweet marjoram, and are therefore easier to grow. Cuttings of marjoram can be taken in early summer and roots can be divided in spring or autumn.

Bay

Bay (*Laurus nobilis*) is a native of the Mediterranean countries and is very slow growing. It has smooth, lanceolate, shiny, leathery, deep green leaves that dry well and have a pungent smell. Small, yellow flowers appear in late spring which, on the female plant, are followed by glossy, blackish berries.

Pot marjoram can be grown for winter use

Bay is slow growing and needs a sheltered position

A perennial, tender, evergreen tree, it can grow to around 9m (30ft) in temperate climates, and is often trained as a standard or a pyramid. It should be planted in a sheltered position in a light, well-drained soil. In cold areas, plant it in a container and overwinter indoors. Bay looks most attractive when grown in a tub: keep it cut back to a central stem and give it a dressing of fertilizer a couple of times a year. Don't allow the soil in the tub to dry out. Young bay trees are planted in autumn or spring; viable seed is virtually impossible to obtain. Heel cuttings can be taken in mid-spring, or half-ripe cuttings in late summer and placed in a cold frame in pots. These can be planted out in a nursery bed during the following autumn where they should remain for two years.

Chervil

Chervil (*Anthriscus cerefolium*) is a hardy biennial, usually grown as an annual. It grows to a height of 50cm (20in). It has small, feathery, green leaves which have a slightly peppery and parsley-like flavour. Umbels of small, white flowers appear from early to late summer. It likes a light, well-drained soil in a sheltered, half-shaded position.

Chervil, which is propagated by seed only, can be sown several times out of doors from late spring to mid-summer for a succession of leafy plants. Seed can also be sown in late summer for indoor winter supplies. The seed should be sown where the herb is to grow, as chervil doesn't like being transplanted. Sow in shallow drills and cover lightly with soil. The seed will germinate very quickly and should be kept moist. Seedlings should be thinned to about 15cm (6in) apart, and the leaves can usually be cut six to eight weeks after sowing. Chervil will quickly run to seed in hot, dry conditions.

Salad burnet

Salad burnet (*Sanguisorba minor*) is a perennial growing to a height of about 45cm (18in). It is a decorative, hardy plant, with a dense rosette of leaves from which stems of small, toothed, green leaves spray out. The young foliage is cucumber scented and lace-like in appearance. The older foliage tastes bitter. The herb has purple-tinted, round

Chervil is enjoyed by salad lovers, eaten fresh

Salad burnet keeps its leaves during winter

heads of tiny, green flowers throughout the summer. Cut the flower stems to ensure a good supply of fresh leaves and to prevent the plant from self-seeding.

Salad burnet is easily grown from seed in mid-spring in an open, sunny position. Thin out the seedlings to 30cm (12in) apart. Established plants can be propagated by division in early spring. Salad burnet keeps its leaves during winter, so it can be used in winter salads.

Sage

There are some 900 species of sage (salvia) which are mostly aromatic and mainly evergreen perennial shrubs and sub-shrubs. Pineapple sage (*Salvia elegans* 'Scarlet Pineapple') with its pointed pineapple-like scented leaves and spikes of red to pink flowers which appear in winter is an evergreen perennial sub-shrub. The white-flowered *Salvia officinalis* 'Albiflore' is extremely elegant, growing to a height of 60–80cm (24–32in), while the compact yellow-leaved sage *Salvia officinalis* 'Kew Gold', just 30cm (12in) high, is a lovely addition to any herb bed or border. Painted sage (*Salvia viridis*), with its erect stems, downy leaves and showy purple bracts, is another delightful addition as is the colourful *Salvia sclarea* var. *turkestanica*.

Sage enjoys a dry, sunny spot, sheltered from the cold wind, preferring a light, well-drained, slightly chalky soil. Once established in the garden, it will produce new branches every year. Two- or three-year-old bushes tend to become straggly, and any new branches should be removed to make new plants.

Sage grows quickly from seed or cuttings and requires little attention

Sage grows quickly from seed or cuttings and needs very little attention. Fresh plants should be planted in a different place; sage doesn't do well if replanted in the same soil. Seed should be sown in mid- to late spring in shallow drills, and lightly covered with soil. Cuttings can be taken from early spring to early autumn, and these will root quickly if given some bottom heat. They can be taken with a 'heel' and planted in an open, sunny position. Sage can also be propagated by layering, the side shoots that have been pinned down rooting in about eight weeks. Alternatively, the herb can be increased by mound layering. Sage will not always survive a hard winter.

Coriander seeds are a delicate spice, used in curries and other Eastern dishes

The flowers of coriander are followed by its seeds

Coriander

Coriander (*Coriandrum sativum*) is a slender annual that grows to about 60cm (24in) in height. The leaves are mid-green and divided, broad at the base of the plant and finer towards the top. The flowers are very pale mauve or pinky-white, and they bloom in clusters from early to late summer. The whole plant has a strong smell about it until the seeds ripen in late summer. The seeds are large, round and yellowish-brown in colour and are where the fragrance is concentrated. Once they have ripened, they develop an agreeable, aromatic perfume similar to honey and oranges.

Seed should be sown in spring in a sunny position and kept well watered to encourage leaf growth from the base. Sow in a free-draining soil where the herb is to grow: coriander doesn't like being transplanted. Germination is quick, and the herb will produce leaves until the first frosts. Seed can also be sown in succession throughout the summer.

Tarragon

Tarragon is a perennial herb that grows to 60cm (2ft) in both height and spread. French tarragon (*Artemisia dracunculus*) is the variety to grow because of its distinctive, delicate flavour. It bears spikes of greenish-yellow flowers in mid- to late summer. Russian tarragon (*Artemisia dracunculoides*) is taller than the French variety, looks very similar, but has coarse, tasteless leaves.

Tarragon has spreading, underground runners which must be given plenty of room. It should be renewed every three years and almost never sets seed in temperate climates. It is propagated by root offshoots and stem cuttings in spring. Pieces of root should be 7.5cm (3in) long and stem cuttings 5cm (2in) in length. The cuttings root readily in a sandy soil.

Tarragon is hard to establish and should be planted in winter when it is dormant. It likes a well-drained soil and sunny position. The sun brings out its full flavour, and it has a stronger flavour if cut often. It will not tolerate a wet soil, preferring a light, fairly dry one, not too rich in fertilizer. Protection should be given in winter, particularly if the plant is young. New, bright green shoots will start to appear in early spring.

Dill

Dill (*Anethum graveolens* also *Peucedanum graveolens*) is a hardy annual rather like fennel to look at, growing to a height of 1m (39in). It has feathery, very finely divided leaves and a hollow stem. Umbels of small, dull, yellow flowers appear in mid- to late summer, to be followed by brown, ridged, aromatic seeds.

Seed should be sown in shallow drills in mid-spring where it is to grow. Sow in rows about 30cm (12in) apart and thin to 22.5cm (9in). A second sowing in mid-summer will produce a further supply in autumn. Germination usually takes around three weeks, depending on the temperature of the soil. Dill likes a light, medium-rich soil with plenty of moisture and grows well in cool conditions and a sheltered spot. The plants will run to seed if they become too dry. If a few plants are allowed to produce flower-heads, the herb will self-seed.

Tarragon is a difficult plant to establish

Dill produces aromatic brown, ridged seeds

Winter savory is a small, woody perennial. Its leaves are particularly aromatic

Savory

There are three types of savory, all of which are similar in flavour. Winter savory (*Satureja montana*) is a small, woody perennial, while summer savory (*Satureja hortensis*) is an annual. Winter savory has thin, dark green, very aromatic leaves. The flowers, which appear in late summer/early autumn can be almost white, pink or pale purple. Winter savory can be grown from seed or propagated by division in spring, or from 5cm (2in) soft tip cuttings taken in late spring. Cut back in spring to keep the herb compact.

Summer savory grows to a height of around 50cm (20in) and has small, pointed green leaves and tiny white or pinkish flowers. The seed should be sown where the plant is to grow in spring, in drills 6mm (¼in) deep. Seedlings should be thinned to 15cm (6in) apart in rows 30cm (12in) apart. Summer savory has a spicy, almost peppery flavour. Both savories will grow in poor, stony soil, provided that it is free-draining.

Creeping winter savory (*Satureja spicigera*) has strongly flavoured, deep green foliage with white flowers about 6mm (¼in) long that appear in late summer and continue into early autumn. It grows to a height of 6cm (2½in) with a spread of 30cm (12in). It is an ideal plant for a herb rockery (see pages 128–9).

Creeping winter savory hugs the ground

USING CULINARY HERBS IN COOKING

Basil

Use in tomato salads and sauces, pesto or pistou sauce, and to make basil vinegar for salads. Chop it into omelettes, or use it in soups. A favourite in Provençal cooking: the French call it *herbe royale*.

Bay

Use the leaves in bouquet garni, pâtés, marinades. Use also in stews, soups and casseroles.

Borage

Young borage leaves, with their cucumber taste, can be used in salads. The blue flowers look good in summer drinks, Pimm's in particular. They can also be scattered over salads for colour, or frozen into ice cubes.

Fennel has fine, feathery leaves and yellow flowers

Chervil

Chervil is best eaten fresh. Chop the leaves into green salads, or mix with a mayonnaise or soured cream dressing for cucumber salads. Add to soups shortly before cooking is completed. Also use in sauces and egg dishes.

Chives

Fresh chives can be snipped over salads, beaten into soft cheeses and added to scrambled eggs, sauces and salad dressings.

Dill

The seed heads can be found in pickled cucumber and the seeds alone take the place of caraway in the breads and cakes of some countries. Fresh dill leaves can be used with fish and in delicate sauces. It freezes well and makes a very good vinegar.

Fennel

Fennel has an aniseed-like flavour and can be used with fish, pork and veal. It is also used in Italian cooking. Freezes and dries well.

Borage flowers appear from early summer onwards

Garlic

Can be added to stews, casseroles, pasta, salads and butters. A touch of garlic is very good in sauces. Pull off single cloves as required, peel, and slice or crush.

Horseradish

A pungent flavour, best known in horseradish sauce made from the finely grated, thick, white roots of the plant. This sauce is very good served with roast beef or fish.

Lemon balm

Lemon balm, with its pungent, lemon-scented leaves, is one of the main ingredients of the liqueur chartreuse. It is delicious in long, cool, summer drinks and in sauces. It makes a wonderfully refreshing tea. Dries and freezes well.

Lovage

The leaves and stems of lovage taste very like celery, but they should be used sparingly as their flavour is strong. Lovage is good added to soups and can be used in salads. The stems can be candied and the seeds added to cream cheese. The leaves dry and freeze well.

Marjoram

There are various varieties of marjoram, all with a slightly sweet, spicy taste. The strength of the taste depends upon where the marjoram is grown, because it is the sun that makes the difference to the pungency of flavour. Wild marjoram tastes slightly bitter and less peppery. Sweet marjoram is less bitter, while pot marjoram has a slightly stronger flavour than the sweet variety. Use in salads, sprinkled over tomatoes, in casseroles, pâtés, sausages and stuffings. Sweet marjoram gives a sweet, mild flavour to dishes, such as pasta and pizza.

Mint

There are many varieties of mint, of which spearmint is the favourite for cooking. Sprinkle fresh mint over salads, and preserve it by making it into mint jelly or mint sauce to serve with lamb. It dries and freezes well.

Parsley

Parsley, often used as a garnish, can be added to fish and white meat dishes, as well as to stuffings, sauces and egg dishes. It is an important ingredient of bouquet garni. It forms the basis of fines herbes, and is an important ingredient of sauces such as vinaigrette, *sauce verte* and *ravigote*. A small bunch can be added to casseroles and stews.

Curly spearmint is an ornamental cultivar

Parsley grows well when its roots are cool

Rosemary

Rosemary has a pungent flavour and is good with lamb, pork, rabbit or game. Use it in marinades, to flavour oils and vinegars and in biscuits or scones. The flowers can be crystallized or used to flavour sugar.

Salad burnet

Salad burnet can be mixed with vegetables in soups, and its fresh, young, cucumber-tasting leaves are good in salads or sandwiches. It can be finely chopped to make a herb butter, and it is an important ingredient of the French sauce, *ravigote*.

Sage

Sage leaves are very aromatic and excellent with poultry and certain meats. The dried, crumbled leaves are good in sage and onion stuffing. When frying liver, add sage to the butter. Its flavour is strong, so use sparingly.

Savory

Summer savory, with its rather bitter flavour, is traditionally cooked with broad beans and peas. It goes well in sausages and stuffings, and can be sprinkled sparingly over salads. It doesn't dry very well but can be frozen.

Sorrel

Young sorrel leaves can be snipped over salads or added to omelettes. They also purée well. Never cook sorrel in an iron pan. If you do, it will develop a metallic taste. Sorrel leaves freeze well for later use.

Sweet cicely

Sweet cicely is a natural sweetener and can be stewed with fruit such as rhubarb or gooseberries, counteracting the acidity of the fruit. It can be used in summer puddings, jellies, mousses and fruit salads. All parts of the plant have a sweetish taste with a hint of aniseed, but the leaves are the part to use.

Tarragon

French tarragon is the variety to use, but it should be used sparingly as it has a strong aniseed flavour. Use it in omelettes, soups and to accompany chicken. It is excellent with scrambled eggs and the leaves can be chopped into salads, stuffings and sauces. French tarragon can be found in mayonnaise, and in Bernaise, Hollandaise and tartare sauces. It is also an ingredient of fines herbes.

Thyme

Common or garden thyme, with its spicy flavour, is excellent in casseroles and soups, and also with root vegetables. It can be mixed with parsley for stuffings, and is also used in pâtés and various kinds of sausages. It is also good with oily fish. Thyme can be dried, but it does not freeze very well.

6 HERBS FOR FRAGRANCE AND COLOUR

A garden designed for fragrance and colour is a source of pleasure for both the gardener who created it and the visitors who delight in its charm. Colour, however, needs to be used with discretion: a dominant colour will only work in contrast with its surroundings. So, for maximum impact, it is sensible to use a predominance of less vibrantly coloured plants which will work best in simple designs. Bear in mind that it is usually colour alone that initially draws the eye to plant combinations, after which texture and form may become apparent.

It is, however, difficult to achieve a note of brilliant colour with herbs. Their shades are mostly low-toned and subtle, which is ideal, as colour in the herb garden needs to be discreet. There are, of course, some flamboyant herbs with vibrant coloured flowers such as vivid red and yellow nasturtiums, bright red poppies, vivid orange marigolds and luscious red peonies.

Yellow Californian poppies are annuals that can be planted in drifts to fill gaps in a mixed border

The perfume of lavender is strongest in its flowers, which are often dried and used to scent linen and clothes

EXAMPLES OF HERBS TO PLANT
Lavender

Lavender makes a delightful mass of colour and its flowers, which are very aromatic, last for weeks. There are many different species and forms of lavender, two of the most common varieties being French lavender (*Lavandula stoechas*) and English lavender (*Lavandula angustifolia*). French lavender forms an attractive shrub with narrow leaves and tight whorls of small, dark purple flowers with purple tufts called bracts. It thrives in light soil, sand or gravel, in a sunny position.

English lavender grows to 60–90cm (24–36in) high, with pointed, narrow, grey leaves and flowers of deep mauve which appear in summer and grow in long spikes. It is ideal for planting as a low hedge. There are other varieties, including *L. dentata*, *L. pinnata*, and the white flowering *L. alba*. Most of the English lavenders, however, are forms or hybrids of *L. angustifolia*. Try growing traditional favourites such as

L. angustifolia 'Loddon Pink' with its vivid green foliage and lilac pink flowers from mid- to late summer, or 'Munstead' with its lavender-blue flowers from early to late summer, or 'Hidcote' with deep, rich violet flowers that bloom also from early to late summer.

All lavenders need full sun, an open position and good drainage as they hate having their roots in water. Seed, which is variable, can be sown from early spring to early summer, but germination can be erratic and slow. It is much better to grow the herb from softwood cuttings taken in mid- to late spring. The cuttings, 10cm (4in) long, should be taken from strong sideshoots and inserted into sandy compost. They are usually slow to root, taking six to eight weeks in spring. Lavender can also be propagated from heel cuttings taken in late summer or early autumn. Keep the plants well trimmed to prevent the herb becoming too woody and straggly in growth.

Pot marigold

Pot marigold (*Calendula officinalis*) is a daisy-like, hardy annual that will grow well when planted in full sun in a well-drained soil. Pot marigolds, which grow to a height of 30–50cm (12–20in), have pale green, oblong, pointed or blunt-tipped leaves which are slightly hairy. The flowers are usually a rich, deep orange or, less commonly, yellow, and bloom throughout the summer months – they are at their peak in late summer – until the first frosts of autumn, if they are regularly dead headed. If you intend to eat the marigolds make sure they are of the *Calendula officinalis* variety. Never eat any member of the *tagetes* species.

Sow the seed 12mm (½in) deep outside in late spring directly into its growing position. Thin the seedlings to 30cm (12in) apart to allow for spreading. Seed can also be sown under glass in mid-spring and the seedlings transplanted. The plants will self-seed if some flower heads are left on.

Pot marigolds overhanging the edge of a border

The leaves of lemon verbena have a strong fragrance

Lemon verbena

Lemon verbena (*Aloysia triphylla*) is a graceful shrub which grows to a height of around 2m (6ft 6in). It has long, tapering, light green leaves and clusters of somewhat insignificant, lemon-scented, pinkish-lilac flowers which appear in late summer. A half-hardy perennial, it is easy to cultivate in a cool climate against a sunny garden wall or in a large pot. Keep it in a large container in cold areas, and, if possible, move it under cover during winter. If left outside, the plant should be cut down and the roots covered with straw. Lemon verbena prefers a light, well-drained soil. A dry, arid soil will help keep it sturdy, but weak, soft, lush growth will result if planted in a richer, moister soil.

In some countries, seed can be difficult to obtain, so stem cuttings, which root quickly, should be taken in late spring or early summer. To plant lemon verbena, dig a planting hole about 30cm (12in) deep in late spring and place the plant in it. Keep the roots well-watered until it establishes itself. Young shoots will appear in early summer when the plant should be lightly pruned to cut out any dead wood, and to shorten some of the shoots so that a good shape is maintained. Harvest lemon verbena in late summer when the plant is at least one year old.

Bergamot

The whole plant of *Monarda didyma* has a lemon-orange scent, and is very attractive to bees, hence its name 'bee balm'. It is a decorative perennial herb standing about 60–90cm (2–3ft) high, with slightly toothed, hairy leaves, and whorls of scarlet, mauve, white or pink flowers from early summer to early autumn. The red-flowering bergamot is known as Oswego tea because, it is said, the Oswego tribe of American Indians brewed a herb tea or tisane from its leaves.

Bergamot is increased by division of its fibrous roots in spring or by cuttings taken in autumn. The roots can be divided every other year, but only the outer shoots of the roots should be used for replanting as the inner part of the established plant tends to die. It can be grown from seed which should be sown in trays in early to mid-spring to a depth of 6mm (¼in), and the seedlings thinned and transplanted when large enough. Bergamot likes a rich, warm, moist soil with a cool root run, so it flourishes best in part shade. Work some compost into the soil before planting.

Cotton lavender

A shrubby perennial (*Santolina chamaecyparissus*) that grows to a height of 30–60cm (12–24in). It has strongly scented, feathery, silver-grey leaves, woolly in texture. The stem is also silvery and woolly, and brownish towards the base. The button-like flowers in a clear lemon yellow appear in mid-summer.

The herb enjoys a fertile, light, well-drained soil in a position of full sun, although it is happy in most soils. It can be grown from semi-ripe cuttings taken in summer, by root division in spring, or by layering the older stems in summer. Pinch out the growing points to keep the plant bushy. Clip back the plants in spring to keep them in shape, and again after flowering. Cotton lavender makes a very good hedge and a suitable edging herb. Plants should be placed about 90cm (3ft) apart.

Bergamot flowers can be white, pink, mauve or scarlet, and the leaves are lemon scented

Cotton lavender is popular as an ornamental shrub and contrasts well with darker hedging plants

Curry plant is effective as an insect repellent

Curry plant

A shrubby perennial (*Helichrysum italicum* syn. *H. angustifolium*) that grows to a height of 60cm (24in) with a spread of 1m (39in). It has strongly pepper-scented, silver foliage and bears yellow button-like flowers in summer. Its scent is strongest after rain. It is only just hardy and thrives in a sunny, sheltered position and a well-drained soil. Seed can be sown in spring and it can also be propagated by stem cuttings in late summer. Protect the roots from frost in colder areas.

Anise hyssop

Anise hyssop (*Agastache foeniculum* syn. *Agastache anethiodora*) is a North American mint that grows to a height of 90cm (3ft).

It is a hardy perennial that dies down every winter. Its pointed leaves, which have a distinct aniseed smell, grow on short stalks and have pale undersides and serrated margins. It bears spikes of pale purple flowers from mid- to late summer. It is mainly ornamental and likes sunny, but cool, weather. Anise hyssop is happy to grow in almost any type of soil and can cope with light shade.

Seed should be sown under cover in spring and softwood cuttings taken in summer. It can be short-lived, so increase your supply from cuttings every two or three years. The herb will self-seed and can be propagated by root division.

Southernwood

Southernwood (*Artemisia abrotanum*) is a small perennial shrub with woody stems and feathery, grey-green leaves, which are downy. It has an aromatic perfume, rather like camphor, and if it flowers – in some countries it doesn't – the yellow-white flowers are small. Also known as 'Lad's Love', it produces long, woody stems and grows to a height of 1.2m (4ft).

It can be grown from softwood cuttings taken in late spring/early summer, or by heel cuttings in autumn. The cuttings will root easily and grow quickly in fine weather. When planting, leave about 38cm (15in) between each plant.

Southernwood should be cut back in spring to two buds of the previous year's growth to promote foliage. It can be planted in any odd spot and is not fussy regarding soil or climate.

Rue

Rue (*Ruta graveolens*) is a hardy perennial that grows to about 60cm (24in) high. It has distinctive, green-blue, finely cut, aromatic leaves and umbels of small, soft yellow flowers. Rue can be grown from seed sown in mid-spring, and the seedlings transplanted when large enough to handle at a distance of about 30cm (12in) apart. The herb can be propagated by stem cuttings in late spring and summer and also by root division. It will also self-seed if allowed to. Clip the plants every alternate spring to encourage bushy growth. Rue is principally a decorative herb – try 'Jackman's Blue', which has much bluer leaves. It can irritate the skin, so always wear gloves when handling it. Large quantities of the leaves can be poisonous.

Decorative rue will grow almost anywhere

Southernwood is a hardy, aromatic shrub

Woodruff

Woodruff (*Galium odoratum*) is a hardy perennial that grows to a height of 15–30cm (6–12in). It has slender, erect, spreading stems and whorls of slightly glossy, green leaves which, when dried, have a scent like new-mown hay. Small, white, star-like flowers appear in late spring. It can be grown from seed sown in mid-spring, 3mm (⅛in) deep in a light, damp, humus-rich soil in light shade. Seed takes a long time to germinate. The herb can be increased by root division in early spring. Young plants should be planted 20cm (8in) apart. Woodruff is a carpeting, ground-cover herb that enjoys being under trees as well as in open borders.

DESIGNING A SCENTED HERB GARDEN

A cottage-garden-type layout is ideal for planting herbs with scented flowers and leaves. By growing a well-chosen variety of fragrant, aromatic herbs, your garden will be redolent with a wide range of scents: aromatic and spicy, sweet and tangy. It will also attract a multitude of butterflies and bees, and each herb will provide colour, form and texture. An aromatic herb garden is the place for scented herbs of all kinds, ranging from roses, honeysuckle, jasmine, mint and rosemary, to sage, lavender and a variety of thymes.

Planning the garden

When planning the garden, consider positioning your herbs on various levels, ranging from arbours, trellises and hanging baskets above, down to chamomile and thyme at your feet. Try also to inject a feeling of seclusion by the use of fencing, hedges or walls to enclose the whole garden and protect it from the wind while allowing its mingled perfumes to hang on the breeze.

Plant a climbing sweet briar rose such as *Rosa eglanteria*, with its apple-scented leaves and

Other herbs for a scented garden

Anise (*Pimpinella anisum*)
Basil (ocimum)
Clary sage (*Salvia sclarea*)
Clove carnation (*Dianthus caryophyllus*)
Cowslip (*Primula veris*)
Cumin (*Cuminum cyminum*)
Lemon balm (*Melissa officinalis*)
Melilot (*Melilotus officinalis*)
Pennyroyal (*Mentha pulegium*)
Rue (*Ruta graveolens*)
Scented-leaf geranium (pelargonium)
Sweet cicely (*Myrrhis odorata*)
Valerian (*Valeriana officinalis*)

pink blossoms or *Rosa rubiginosa* with its smell of stewed apples. The rich, sweet fragrance of the pink rambler 'Albertine' is also hard to beat. For fragrance and ease of cultivation, grow the *Rosa rugosa* roses. They will not only scent the air, but will produce huge hips full of vitamin C for making rosehip jam or syrup.

You might also like to grow clematis: *Clematis flammula* or 'Fragrant Bower' is quite beautiful with large clusters of creamy

A white Rugosa rose with dark green divided leaves

Rose hips are both decorative and useful

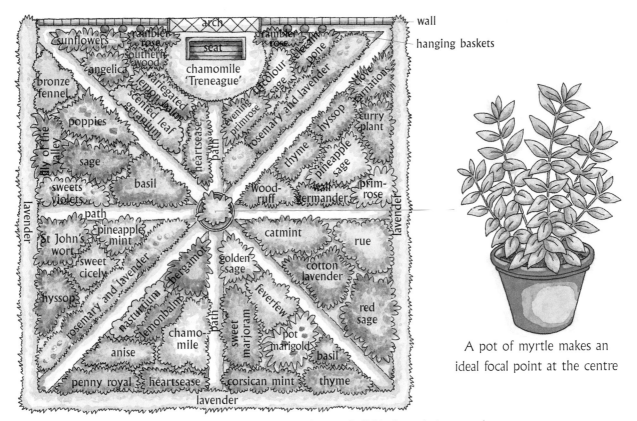

A design for a scented herb garden, where fragrant plants of all kinds and sizes can be grown

A pot of myrtle makes an ideal focal point at the centre

white flowers and a delightful, sweet perfume.

Herbs come in a succession of lovely colours. The earliest to bloom are rosemary, the purple and white violets, and lungwort with its soft rose colour. Later come the yellow star flowers of the shrubby St John's wort, the rich sapphire of hyssop and the scarlet of bergamot, while the purple bronze of red sage (*Salvia officinalis* 'Purpurascens Group') and the pretty, white daisies of chamomile lend emphasis to the delicacy of pink and white foxgloves. All of these plants can grow in harmony with aromatic, sweet-scented herbs such as marjoram; savory; green, silver and gold thyme; the velvety sages and the lavenders.

Any herb garden cultivated for its scent and colour will need a number of paths and small beds, somewhere to sit, with pots or raised beds near the seat. Use trellis and

Foxgloves, although poisonous, are eye-catching

Pineapple mint has pretty, variegated foliage

arbours as support for climbing jasmines, hops and honeysuckles. The giant honeysuckle, *Lonicera hildebrandiana* creates the perfect foil for pink roses. Hedges of sweet briar, old roses, lavender, rosemary and cotton lavender will ensure that every part of the garden is sweetly perfumed.

Base your garden around the greys and greens of the most shrubby, aromatic herbs. Flowering herbs such as hyssop, scarlet bergamot, yellow elecampane, evening primrose and meadowsweet (*Filipendula ulmaria*) can then be planted amongst them. Creeping thyme, creeping chamomile with its fruity scent, and prostrate mints such as Corsican mint (also known as woolly mint, *Mentha requienii*) or applemint (*Mentha suaveolens*) can be grown in the cracks between paving stones or in gravel paths. Borders of violets and double-flowered chamomile can line paths and 'pour' over them. Shrubby artemisias and catmints, interwoven with woodruff and variegated pineapple mint, can also be planted.

It is always important to ensure that you have a seasonal balance of herbs. Evergreens such as rosemary, lavender, box and bay will ensure greenery all year round. For spring colour, bronze fennel, *Foeniculum vulgare* 'Purpureum', produces feathery, bronze-coloured foliage from early spring. Or try lovage, with its parsley-like flowers and soft green, divided leaves. Angelica, primroses, sweet violets and lily of the valley also make welcome springtime visitors.

The myrtle, *Myrtus communis* 'Flore Pleno', will flower into the autumn, and pineapple sage (*Salvia elegans* 'Scarlet Pineapple') will produce rich spikes of scarlet flowers during winter. The autumn crocus, *Colchicum autumnale*, has lilac or purple flowers, and the tall sunflower, *Helianthus annuus*, with its colourful blooms of cream, yellow or gold, will flower well into the autumn, as will bergamot and lemon verbena.

Bronze fennel grows up to 2m (6ft 6in) tall

HERBS THAT ATTRACT BEES AND BUTTERFLIES

All herb gardens make a feeding paradise for bees and butterflies because herbs are usually highly perfumed and rich in nectar. These insects depend upon a wide selection of plants for their survival, and herbs, with their strong scents and simple flowers, attract them. It is hardly surprising that a bee hive was often the centrepiece of medieval herb gardens and that, traditionally, various herbs were grown around it, although bees will forage for up to half a mile from the hive.

Attracting bees

The herb garden should be in full sun to attract bees, and herbs should be planted in groups of five or six. Bees don't like being buffeted by the wind, so some sort of windbreak, such as a hedge or trellis, should be provided to shelter the site.

To encourage bees, plant the herbs that they love, such as bergamot – known as 'bee balm', poppies, mint, heartsease, edgings of catmint and borage, and box. Bees also love the flowers of sage, thyme, lavender, mint, hyssop and rosemary. Always choose those herbs that will provide nectar and pollen for the longest possible time. Herbs such as hyssop, fennel, sage, basil, horehound, rosemary, the marjorams and mints and both summer and winter savory will supply nectar throughout the season when bees are foraging.

Contented bees need a succession of such

As well as the more traditional herbs, bees enjoy the large, striking flowers of the sunflower plant

plants and, even in winter, snowdrops, crocus and lungwort will provide nectar for bees that leave hibernation early. The wallflower, which used to be called 'bee flower', is among the best of spring bee herbs, and primroses and cowslips are also popular. Anise hyssop is an important bee plant, and Korean mint (*Agastache rugosa*) is worth cultivating. You could grow calamint, which flowers from mid-summer to mid-autumn, and autumn crocus, which will provide nectar from early to late autumn.

Provide the garden with hellebores in early spring. A hedge of holly and ivy will supply nectar flowers in both spring and autumn. Foxgloves have adapted their flowers to attract bees: the spots in their throats lead the bees to the nectar.

Marigolds attract bees and other beneficial insects

Bergamot is a favourite herb with bees

Other herbs for the bee garden

Basil (ocimum)

Comfrey (*Symphytum officinale*)

Dyer's bugloss (*Alkanna tinctoria*)

Evening primrose (*Oenothera biennis*)

Fennel (*Foeniculum vulgare*)

Feverfew (*Tanacetum parthenium* formerly *Chrysanthemum*)

German chamomile (*Matricaria recutita*)

Lavenders (lavandula)

Meadowsweet (*Filipendula ulmaria*)

Mullein (*Verbascum thapsus*)

Musk mallow (*Malva moschata*)

Poppy (papaver)

Purple loosestrife (*Lythrum salicaria*)

Sages (salvia)

Savory (satureja)

Tansy (*Tanacetum vulgare*)

Vervain (*Verbena officinalis*)

Yarrow (*Achillea millefolium*)

Herbs for a butterfly garden

Butterfly nectar plants
Bugle (*Ajuga reptans*)
Carnation (dianthus)
Coltsfoot (*Tussilago farfara*)
Heartsease (*Viola tricolor*)
Honeysuckle (lonicera)
Lavender (lavandula)
Marjoram (origanum)
Musk mallow (*Malva moschata*)
Purple loosestrife (*Lythrum salicaria*)
Rosemary (*Rosmarinus officinalis*)
St John's wort (*Hypericum perforatum*)
Thymes (thymus)
Valerian (*Valeriana officinalis*)
Yarrow (*Achillea millefolium*)

Herbs for butterfly larvae
The butterfly lays its eggs on these plants.
The eggs become larvae and the larvae,
depending on the species of butterfly, feed
on either the leaves or flowers of the plants.

Cowslip (*Primula veris*)
Fennel (*Foeniculum vulgare*)
Foxglove (*Digitalis purpurea*)
Horseradish (*Armoracia rusticana*)
Musk mallow (*Malva moschata*)
Nettles (*Urtica dioica*)
Rocket (*Eruca vesicaria* subsp. *sativa*)
Sweet violet (*Viola odorata*)
Wild strawberry (*Fragaria vesca*)

Attracting butterflies

Butterflies are more attracted by scent than colour, preferring faded colours. They love marigolds, garden pinks and rocket (*Eruca vesicaria* subsp. *sativa*) but, most of all, they love buddleia. Butterflies enjoy single herbs with flat heads of blossom, such as purple loosestrife (*Lythrum salicaria*), rocket and catmint (*Nepeta cataria*), and they are attracted to the flowers of old English lavender. Borage is a favourite food of the Painted Lady butterfly. Knapweeds (centaurea) are also good butterfly nectar plants and food for this species. Orange Tip butterflies will feed on the cuckoo flower (*Cardamine pratensis*). Self heal (*Prunella vulgaris*) is worth growing while vervain (*Verbena officinalis*) in flower is another notable butterfly herb. A basket of herbs containing mint and chives in flower will attract both butterflies and bees.

Butterflies love to feed on *Buddleia davidii*

HERBS TO GROW IN THE FLOWER BORDER

The traditional approach to mixed borders, consisting of herbs and other garden plants, usually means using complementary or toning colours, but mixing 'hot' and 'cool' colours in large, natural drifts is becoming increasingly popular.

A mixed border can be made by planting a number of hardy perennials that bring a series of gentle changes throughout the growing season, and which have fragrant foliage or perfumed flowers, with herbs that will complement both them and the border. Perennials should be used as much for their foliage as for their flowers. Annuals can be used both in drifts, and to fill any gaps. Try Californian poppies (*Eschscholzia californica*), nasturtiums, marigolds and love-in-the-mist (*Nigella damascena*). For background interest, plant shrubs and small trees.

Siting a mixed border

The siting of a mixed border is important, as most perennials and annuals only flourish in full sunlight: they need a sunny site to make hard growth. If your site is overshadowed by trees or buildings, St John's wort and the periwinkles (*Vinca major* and *Vinca minor*) all thrive in shade. These plants require little attention, with periwinkle bearing bright blue flowers in spring. Take care, though, as it spreads rapidly and could suffocate neighbouring plants.

Generally speaking, the majority of plants will thrive in a light, well-drained soil, into which has been worked a small quantity of organic matter.

Chamomile flourishing at the front of a mixed border

Care must be taken when mixing heights of plants, as otherwise some can be lost in the middle

Arranging the plants

When planting your border, plant in groups of three or five plants of one variety in an irregular shape for the greatest impact and to create marvellous splashes of colour. Plant the taller species at the back, allowing plenty of room for them to spread, and then graduate the plant heights so that the smallest ones are at the front. Remember that your plants should always be suited to their position in the border and to the type of soil. Never mix together plants of differing heights or the smaller ones will be 'lost'.

Aim to create year-round interest for the best effect, with decorative shrubs or trees providing the main intercst. Try using plants with variegated or evergreen foliage. Consider carefully how to harmonize the colour combinations – that includes leaf colour as well as flower shades. Draw a planting plan on paper, marking in the position of each plant you choose. If you make a mistake, the plants can easily be moved around.

Sunflowers, such as the upright *Helianthus annuus* 'Lemon Queen' with its pale yellow, daisy-like flowers, will add brightness in early autumn. It grows to a height of 1.8m (6ft) and spreads to 1m (39in) so it is ideal to plant at the back of the border. Angelica, bay, rosemary, fennel and lovage make a good backdrop for a mixed border. The clump-forming evergreen achillea, *Achillea filipendulina*, with its flat, golden yellow flower heads from its second year onwards, is also ideal as it grows to a height of 1.2m (4ft), with a 45cm (18in) spread. Be sure to dead head the plants to encourage a second flush of blooms.

Pink lavatera will thrive in a sunny border

The colours of marigold and curry plant mix well

Pink lavatera and phlox will thrive in a sunny border. Try planting blue-flowering catmint in front of them. Visually imposing plants, such as fennel, tansy and hollyhocks, can be repeated at varying intervals. Bronze fennel (*Foeniculum vulgare* 'Purpureum') is an attractive contrast to pinks and purples or among white and yellow flowers. Near the back of the border you could plant golden rod (*Solidago virgaurea*), which has lanceolate leaves and ruffled, yellow, daisy-like flowers in late summer. The tall perennials which bloom mostly in mid-summer make useful additions to the back or middle of the border: for example, yarrow, hollyhock (*Alcea rosea*), purple loosestrife and the tall, bearded iris, *Iris germanica*.

Pale yellows will cool 'hot' schemes of reds and oranges and gently contrast with blues and mauves. Grey foliage plants with aromatic leaves include lavender, species of artemisia and rue (*Ruta graveolens* 'Jackman's Blue'). Curry plant has silvery, curry-scented leaves with yellow flowers from mid-summer to early autumn. It is a shrubby perennial that grows to a height of 60cm (24in) and

can be planted next to a path, so that the perfume is released every time you rub against it. Cotton lavender has silver-grey leaves and small cream to yellow flowers in mid- to late summer. It grows to a height of 50cm (20in) and is very decorative. All of these, when integrated together, create magnificent foliage combinations.

Camphor plant (*Balsaminta major* var. *tomentosum*) has a lovely camphor scent, silver leaves and white, daisy-like flowers. Jerusalem sage (*Phlomis fruticosa*) is another ornamental plant for the border, with its aromatic, silver leaves and whorls of orange-yellow flowers from early to late summer. It reaches a height of 1.5m (5ft) and is good planted near the back.

Mexican orange (*Choisya ternata*) is an evergreen shrub worth considering. It grows to a height of 3m (9ft 9in) and bears clusters of white flowers at any time of the year, but, in the main, from early to late spring. It is very ornamental and its flowers have a sweet, vanilla-like perfume. Its leaves also have a pleasant, aromatic scent. Musk mallow (*Malva moschata*) is another delightful, bushy, border perennial that grows to a height of around 60cm (2ft) and bears spikes of large, single, pink or white flowers from mid-summer until early autumn. The mid-green leaves, kidney-shaped near the base, emit a musky aroma when pressed and in warm weather.

English garden designer Gertrude Jekyll (1843–1932) created cool blue and grey borders, although true blues are difficult to find in herb plants. There are, however, blue-flowered herbs such as hyssop, flax (*Linum usitatissimum*), lavender and borage. There are many shades of violet and lilac that harmonize beautifully with the greys and silvers of rue, artemisia and lavender.

When designing a mixed border, foliage should be teamed together for effect and flowering plants arranged so that neighbouring species do not all flower at the same time. Where space allows, taller, shrubby herbs such as elder (*Sambucus nigra*), with its many attractive variegated forms, and witch hazel (*Hamamelis virginiana*) can also

Feverfew growing in a mixed flower border

be planted. If you intend to grow a wide range of culinary herbs in the mixed border, remember to leave spaces for some annuals.

Sage is suitable for the middle of the border, but keep it regularly trimmed back. There are several varieties such as tricolour sage (*Salvia officinalis* var. *tricolor*) and purple-leaved sage (*Salvia officinalis* 'Purpurascens'). Invasive herbs such as mint and lemon balm can also be grown, but make sure that they are contained (see page 54). Try growing applemint (*Mentha suaveolens*), the purple-tinted black peppermint (*Mentha piperita* var. *rubra*) and ginger mint (*Mentha* x *gracilis* 'Variegata'). Tarragon can also be planted in this way. You could also cultivate marigolds, scented-leaf geraniums and nasturtiums. Or why not try growing some of the more unusual herbs such as fenugreek (*Trigonella foenum-graecum*), chervil, coriander and anise?

Elecampane, clary sage and sweet cicely are among the finest border plants, and groups of herbs which include chives, marjoram and poppies will provide a marvellous splash of colour. Use the neat, low-growing marjoram for an attractive edging, or chives which can be allowed to bloom when used this way.

An attractive combination of sages

7 HERB LAWNS AND SEATS, PATHS AND PAVING

MAKING A CHAMOMILE LAWN

Chamomile lawns, with their rich, fruity, apple scent, have been popular since medieval times and they produce a smooth, green sward, even on the poorest soil in the driest summer. Unlike grass, however, the surface isn't even, weeds can be a problem and occasionally the lawns can look patchy. Nevertheless, they are an interesting addition to a garden and well worth both the time and the effort that goes into creating them.

Chamaemelum nobile 'Treneague' is the best variety of chamomile to plant for a lawn as it doesn't flower and it produces a low, compact turf. It also tolerates dry conditions.

'Treneague' is propagated from divisions, and it roots where the stems touch the soil. It does best in a sandy, well-drained soil in an open site. It is best to obtain this variety of chamomile from a specialist herb nursery.

Planting a chamomile lawn

A chamomile lawn won't survive wear and tear as turf does, so do not plant a large area. Try planting a small patch which can be square, oblong, or even circular.

Chamomile 'Treaneague' is planted at 10cm (4in) intervals, so it may help to draw a plan first, to calculate the number of plantlets needed (see Stage 5, next page).

A large, lush, chamomile lawn has a textured turf that makes an interesting alternative to grass

You will need:
Ball of string
Short wooden stakes or pegs
Spade
Humus/organic matter (see page 7),
   or grit
Fertilizer
Rake
Tray
Chamomile plants

A chamomile plant, before division

STAGE 1: Mark off the plot with pegs or stakes and string pulled taut.

STAGE 2: Dig the area to one spade's depth, unless the ground is badly compacted, and then remove all weeds, stones and debris. If your soil is light, add compost or manure as you go along. Heavy soil will benefit from the addition of some grit. Level the area with the back of your spade to ensure that firming is even.

STAGE 3: Tread down the soil using your heels, and apply a light dressing of a general fertilizer.

STAGE 4: Rake the soil level, removing any remaining stones.

STAGE 5: Remove each chamomile plant from its container and pull gently at the rootball, dividing it into two pieces. Divide the plant again, to make about three or four smaller plantlets. Each plantlet needs to have good roots.

STAGE 6: Place the plantlets in a tray as you divide them, and cover with moist compost to keep them damp.

STAGE 7: Plant the chamomile at 10cm (4in) intervals, water in well.

Maintenance

Keep the plot well watered. Once the plants have established themselves and knitted together, most weeds will be suppressed. The lawn can then be walked on but will not survive heavy traffic, and can be clipped over lightly with shears. To stop gaps appearing, cut back the chamomile at regular intervals. Roll or tread occasionally to keep all the plants compact.

Chamomile 'Treneague' becoming established

THYME AND PENNYROYAL LAWNS

Thyme

The hardy, creeping thyme, *Thymus serpyllum*, makes an excellent herb lawn with its pleasant perfume when crushed, and the lovely, green, mat effect it produces. Try *Thymus drucei* 'Albus' with its yellow-green leaves and white flowers, and *T. drucei* 'Lanuginosus' which has pale, downy leaves but seldom flowers.

All creeping varieties – *Thymus serpyllum*,

established themselves. This takes about three weeks. When the seedlings have at least two sets of leaves, thin to about 7.5cm (3in). Thin at intervals as the seedlings develop, until the required spacing of 23cm (9in) is reached.

Thyme lawns do not need clipping, but snip off any dead flower heads and stalks in spring as they can help to protect the plants during winter. Once established, thyme makes a fragrant carpet, but it will not tolerate heavy traffic. Keep the lawn well-watered and weed it regularly.

Striking thyme 'Ruby Glow' has a creeping habit

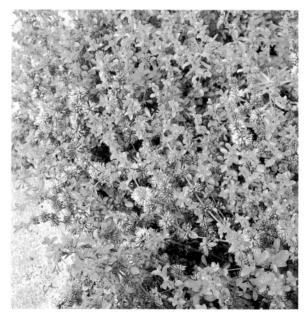

Pennyroyal, one of the mints, is a vigorous grower

T. praecox and *T. pseudolanuginusus* – are suitable for lawn cultivation, but they prefer dry, sandy soil. Select thymes either according to their leaf colour – gold, variegated, grey, dark or light green – or to their flower colour – white, mauve, pink or red. Creeping thyme should be planted at 23cm (9in) intervals.

If you choose to use seed, prepare the area and sow the seed broadcast (see page 43). Water well and keep moist until the seedlings have

Pennyroyal

Pennyroyal (*Mentha pulegium*), with its bright green leaves and pungent scent, is a very satisfactory herb for lawns, as it produces a thick mat of growth that acts as a weed suppressant. It spreads very quickly, is extremely hardy, and bears a profusion of small spires of lavender-coloured flowers in spring. To propagate, roots can be divided in autumn and spring and planted 15–23cm (6–9in) apart.

HERB SEATS

A herb seat built in a sunny, sheltered spot, with an attractive vista, is an ideal place to grow chamomile and creeping thymes – thyme is quick draining while chamomile holds moisture for longer periods of time.

Think carefully when siting your seat. Decide when you are most likely to use it and whether you want to catch the sun early in the day or in the late afternoon.

Sweet-scented herbs can be planted close to the seat – try lavender, lemon verbena, clove carnations (*Dianthus caryophyllus*) and pineapple sage (*Salvia elegans* 'Scarlet Pineapple').

A herb seat can accommodate as many people as you wish; it can be short enough for just two, or it can run the whole length of a wall or fence. Place a few large, flat stones on the seat to sit on during inclement weather. The seat should be positioned so that the sitter faces into the herb garden and, if possible, should be in a position to catch the sun. Cover the fence or wall behind with honeysuckle, jasmine or rambler roses. Try

placing a simple arch over the seat to make an arbour, and plant it with scented climbers – honeysuckle will cover it in just a few seasons. Scented geraniums, lemon balm and various mints can be grown in pots nearby.

Constructing a herb seat

You will need:
Bricks or blocks
Hardcore
Cement, sand and gravel, or ready-mixed
   concrete
Spirit level
Trowel
Piece of wood with a right-angle
Short wooden stakes or pegs
Ball of string
Spade
Hammer
Stone chisel
Builders' retaining wall-ties: 1 per corner
   per layer

STAGE 1: Select your site and draw your plan to scale on paper, marking in the length, height and width of the seat, and position of the bricks. An ideal height for a comfortable seat is 45cm (18in).

STAGE 2: Calculate the number of bricks required, remembering to allow a 12mm (½in) space between the bricks for cement. Also calculate how much hardcore and cement, sand and gravel you will need for the concrete. Ready-mixed concrete is available if preferred.

STAGE 3: Outline the area for your seat with pegs and string pulled taut, using the right-angled piece of wood at the corners.

A newly constructed herb seat within a herb garden

STAGE 4: Using the string as a guideline, dig a trench to a depth of 23cm (9in) by the width of the spade.

STAGE 5: Fill the trench with 15cm (6in) of hardcore and compact it by treading it down, or tamping it down with the blunt end of a piece of timber. Then level it off.

STAGE 6: Top the hardcore with a 7.5cm (3in) layer of concrete, level it off and allow it to set.

STAGE 7: Mix the cement and spread a layer 12mm (½in) thick on top of the concrete to ensure that the bricks adhere to the base.

STAGE 8: Take the first brick and, using a trowel, put 12mm (½in) of cement on the leading end. Lay it on the bed of cement, making sure that it's level by using the spirit level. The line of bricks should run down the centre of the concrete/hardcore foundation.

STAGE 9: Repeat with the next brick, pressing it firmly against the cement on the end of the preceeding brick and so on along the length of the seat.

STAGE 10: Use the right-angled piece of wood to make sure that the corner of the seat is at right angles, and lay the bricks to the width of the seat.

STAGE 11: Continue with the other side and end, until the rectangle is complete.

STAGE 12: Repeat the process for the second layer, laying at least 12mm (½in) of the cement to cover the top of the bottom bricks. Using the trowel, put a 12mm (½in) layer of concrete on the end of the brick and bed it on top of the already laid cement. Centre the brick over a join in the bottom layer for strength.

STAGE 13: If you are not using standard bricks, you will have to halve a brick to complete a row. Use a stone chisel to mark and weaken the halfway line and then break it with a firm blow from the hammer. Alternatively, if you are using standard bricks, the brick used to turn the corner will both complete the row and give the brickwork the necessary strength.

STAGE 14: For non-standard bricks, use builders' retaining wall-ties at each corner for strength, embedding them in the freshly laid cement of each layer. (These are not necessary for standard bricks as they interlock at the corners for strength.)

STAGE 15: Repeat the process to complete the outer shell. If the weather is bad, cover the shell until the cement has set.

STAGE 16: Once the cement has set, the seat is ready for filling (see page 77).

STAGE 17: Plant Roman chamomile (*Chamaemelum nobile*) at a distance of 15cm (6in) apart. It has a height of 15cm (6in) and spread of 45cm (18in), and produces side-shoots, so will spread and form a mat-like carpet. Its yellow-centred, white petalled flowers, rather like a daisy, appear from mid-summer to early autumn. There is also a double-flowered variety, if preferred.

The herb seat planted with chamomile

The herb seat two months later

LAYING PATHS

The width of a path can be anything from 60cm (2ft) to 1.5–1.8m (5–6ft). Usually 1m (39in) is about right, because it is wide enough for wheelchair access and for two people to walk side by side. A path should not be less than 60cm (2ft) to be able to walk in comfort. The path should be level and non-slippery, and it should link various features around the garden. Plan your path carefully to obtain maximum impact.

When laying paths and paving, you should consider what materials are available that will complement your plants and other paved features in your garden. Paths and paving can dominate a garden design and the best choice is usually a discreet, natural surface that blends well with existing plantings.

A concrete path may sound dull and boring, but it is probably the safest as it can have a slightly rippled surface, not only to give a better grip for walking on, but making it ideal for wheelchair tyres. Concrete paths can look rather bland, so make sure that they always lead to some sort of focal point: a sundial, a bird bath or a potted bay, for example. The lay of the land should also be taken into account. On a gentle slope, the path may be laid to follow it, but, if the ground falls away steeply, it is better to construct level sections making a step every 4.6m (15ft) or so.

A discreet, natural path of stone slabs. It blends well with the surrounding plantings, hedging and shrubs, and leads to the restful focal point

Laying a concrete path

STAGE 1: Mark out the area of the path with pegs and string pulled taut. Remove loose surface soil and grass.

(You may wish to dig down several inches to accommodate the depth of both the hardcore and concrete, so that the finished path is level with the ground surface.)

STAGE 2: Spread hardcore 2.5–5cm (1–2in) deep over the area and roll thoroughly to give a solid base.

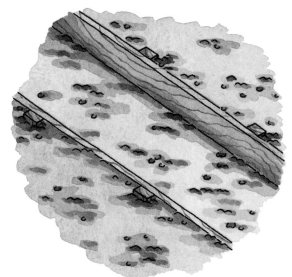

STAGE 3: Lay boards on their long edges each side of the path, using a spirit level, to the depth of the concrete required – usually 5–7.5cm (2–3in) – and secure with pegs driven with the mallet into the ground on the outside of the boards.

STAGE 4: Either buy ready-mixed concrete or mix your own in a ratio of one part cement, two parts sand and three parts gravel. Use a bucket as a measure and add just over half a bucket of water. Mix on a piece of board with a spade, and once it is ready, lay the concrete as soon as possible.

You will need:
Short wooden stakes or pegs
Ball of string
Hardcore
2 boards: 2m (6ft 6in) long (max) x
    7.5cm (3in) wide x 2.5cm (1in) thick
Concrete
Roller
Spade
Mallet
Garden rake
Straight-edged length of wood, a little
    longer than the width of the path
Bucket
Hard brush

STAGE 5: Lay the concrete over the hardcore, working it well into the side boards with a garden rake, a section at a time. Level off with the straight-edged length of wood.

STAGE 6: To give the appearance of gravel, brush the surface with a hard brush about an hour after laying, then again a little later, so that the gravel sits slightly above the surface.

STAGE 7: Allow the path to set hard before walking on it. Always cover with waterproof sheeting if it rains, or if rain is forecast.

Laying a crazy-paving path

Paths made of crazy paving have an informality which looks marvellous with herbs overflowing the borders.

STAGE 1: Mark out the path with pegs and string pulled taut. Remove at least 5cm (2in) of the topsoil and grass, as well as any loose soil, stones and weeds.

STAGE 2: Spread a layer of sifted soil over the area to a depth of 5cm (2in), and then rake over the whole surface until it is perfectly level. Use a spirit level.

STAGE 3: Using the string and pegs as a guide, ensure that the outside edges of your path are even by laying pieces of paving stone with at least one fairly straight edge.

A crazy-paving path has an organic feel

STAGE 4: When fitting the stones, give them two or three gentle taps with a wooden rammer to set them into position. Work systematically along the width and the length of the path.

STAGE 5: Place a little soil under one corner of any pieces of stone that don't lie flat. Make sure that each piece of stone is level with the adjacent one. Some pieces of stone will be thinner than others, so pack with soil as necessary.

STAGE 6: Crazy paving paths usually sink a little after a while, so make your level slightly higher than the surrounding soil or grass to allow for this.

STAGE 7: Fill any crevices and spaces with loose compost to allow for the planting of creeping herbs.

Laying a gravel path

You will need:
Short wooden stakes or pegs
Ball of string
Spade
Hardcore
Sand
Gravel
Roller

STAGE 1: Try to select a site where only the minimum amount of soil will have to be removed to level it. Then mark out the path using the stakes or pegs and lengths of string pulled taut.

STAGE 2: Remove at least 15cm (6in) of topsoil from the path's area.

STAGE 3: Place a 10cm (4in) layer of hardcore over the prepared area.

STAGE 4: Add a thin layer of sand on top.

STAGE 5: Finish the path with a 5cm (2in) layer of gravel. Roll the gravel well in order to compact the stones.

STAGE 6: You will need to roll the path occasionally to keep it level and top it up with more gravel if it is in constant use. Remember also that regular weeding will be necessary.

A gravel path is easy to construct, and will link various features around the garden. It will also give safe and easy access to your herbs, whatever the weather

LAYING PAVING

STAGE 1: Draw your plan to scale showing the size of the area and drawing the paving slabs according to the size on the plan. This will determine how many slabs you will need, but remember to allow for a few breakages.

STAGE 2: Mark out the area to be paved with pegs and string pulled taut, using your plan as a guide.

STAGE 3: Remove about 15cm (6in) of topsoil from between the string to clear the area of grass and weeds.

STAGE 4: Place the hardcore over the area and compact it to the required level with a rammer, filling in any empty spaces with sharp sand and compacting it again.

A paved path bordered by low box hedges

You will need:
Paving slabs of your chosen size and colour
Short wooden stakes or pegs
Ball of string
Spade / fork
Hardcore
Rammer
Sharp sand
12mm- (1/2in)-thick piece of wood
Wooden mallet
Sand

STAGE 5: Remember that any paving next to house walls should lie below the damp course, and below any air bricks that may be present. Also, the paved area should slope slightly away from the building to allow for adequate drainage.

STAGE 6: Start in one corner and lay a 2.5cm (1in) layer of sand over the compacted hardcore, allowing for two paving slabs at a time.

STAGE 7: Place the paving slabs on the sand and tap them down with a wooden mallet to the required level. Allow a 12mm (½in) gap between them, using the 12mm- (½in)-thick piece of wood as a measure.

STAGE 8: Continue in this way until the whole area is covered, using a spirit level to check the line and the level of the slabs as they are laid.

STAGE 9: Some of the gaps between the slabs can be filled with a mixture of sharp sand and compost in which low-growing herbs or herb seed can be planted. Other gaps can be filled with mortar.

Bricks used for paving can be laid in a variety of regular patterns

Herringbone patterns

Herringbone patterns can be used for both paths and larger paved areas. Between the herringbone bricks and those laid first to form a straight edge, there will be a narrow border in which compact herbs can be grown.

STAGE 1: Mark out the area to be paved with pegs and string pulled taut.

STAGE 2: Clear the ground and remove about 15cm (6in) of topsoil.

STAGE 3: Level this off and compact a layer of hardcore into the earth.

STAGE 4: Spread a layer of concrete over this and place the bricks on the smooth surface, laying them to form a straight line along the outside edges of the area.

STAGE 5: Lay the bricks in a herringbone style to form a zig-zag pattern. Use a wooden mallet to gently tap the bricks level, and check with the spirit level.

You will need:
Short wooden stakes or pegs
Ball of string
Spade
Hardcore
Concrete
Bricks
Mallet
Spirit level

The zig-zag pattern of herringbone bricks provides visual interest, especially in a large area

HERBS THAT TOLERATE TREADING

Corsican mint (*Mentha requienii*) forms a close, emerald carpet and when walked on or bruised gives off a strong scent of crème de menthe. The small, wild, lady's mantle, *Alchemilla mollis*, tolerates a certain amount of crushing underfoot, as do the calamints, chamomile and the creeping thymes. You could also try planting the fully hardy *Thymus vulgaris* 'Silver Posie'. Its lovely scent is released when trodden on, and it has small, white-margined leaves and pale mauve-pink flowers appearing in spring and early summer. Remember that although these herbs will tolerate a certain amount of treading, they should not be constantly walked upon.

Thymus vulgaris 'Silver Posie' has a lovely scent

CREEPING HERBS

There are various low-growing, mat-forming herbs which are extremely useful in the herb garden. These plants are quite vigorous, making their growth by spreading outwards, and they not only fill spaces with foliage and flowers, but they also add shape and texture.

Roman chamomile and the various thymes are ideal plants. Other herbs with a creeping or compact habit are pennyroyal and the calamints. *Calamintha alpina*, for example, is an aromatic mat former, but should be planted in the widest crevices possible. It throws up vast numbers of short spikes of fine violet blossom in early or mid-summer, and it forms a luscious, evergreen mat. The calamint also known as basil thyme (*Acinos arvensis*) with its strong, menthol scent, grows to 10cm (4in) tall. It can be planted between paving in dry conditions. It bears blue and purple flowers which, with the leaves, give forth a rich, minty perfume when they are crushed or after a summer shower.

Creeping thymes

Thymus serpyllum 'Hartington Silver' (formerly 'Highland Cream') is a hardy evergreen with bright green leaves edged with cream, bearing pale pink flowers in early to mid-summer. This variegated thyme grows to a height of 5cm (2in) and forms a low, dense mat. It enjoys full sun and a well-drained soil.

Thymus serpyllum 'Goldstream' has thin strands of narrow, lemon-scented, green-gold, variegated leaves and grows to a height of 5cm (2in). It thrives in a sunny position and a well-drained, slightly alkaline soil.

T. serpyllum 'Ruby Glow' is an attractive creeping thyme growing to a height of 10cm (4in), with aromatic, dark green leaves and large, dark crimson flowers. Grow it in a sunny place in a well-drained soil.

Thyme 'Doone Valley' has a citrus scent

Creeping Jenny or Moneywort

A prostrate perennial (*Lysimachia nummularia* 'Aurea') with creeping, rooting stems bearing bright golden foliage which turns greenish-yellow or green in dense shade. It grows to a height of 2.5–5cm (1–2in) with an indefinite spread. Yellow, cup-like flowers appear during summer.

Creeping Jenny spreads extensively

Thymus drucei 'Doone Valley' grows to a height of 15cm (6in) and spreads to 20–30cm (8–12in). It has citrus-scented, golden, variegated leaves, and masses of small, pale purple flowers appear in summer. It enjoys a well-drained, sunny position.

    Thymus serpyllum 'Minor' has pink flowers.

    T. serpyllum coccineus has crimson flowers.

    T. serpyllum 'Snowdrift' has white flowers.

    T. serpyllum 'Lemon Curd' has pink flowers.

Creeping savory

Creeping savory (*Satureja spicigera*) is a hardy, compact, perennial growing to a height of 6cm (2½in). Its leaves are strongly aromatic, and it bears small, white flowers from late summer to early autumn. It thrives in a sunny position and well-drained soil.

Creeping mints

Applemint or woolly mint (*Mentha suaveolens*) is a creeping, downy perennial that grows to a height of 40cm–1m (16–39in), with an indefinite spread. It has a spearmint flavour and a slight apple smell. Corsican mint (*Mentha requienii*) is a tiny, mat-forming perennial with a pungent scent and small lilac flowers that appear in summer. It has an indefinite spread and reaches a height of 2–10cm (¾–4in). Creeping pennyroyal (*Mentha pulegium* 'Cunningham Mint') with its light green leaves, oval in shape, grows to a height of 10–15cm (4–6in) and has an indefinite spread. It enjoys a damp, fertile soil.

MAT-FORMING HERBS

Thymus serpyllum 'Snowdrift': a mat-forming, vigorous thyme that grows to a height of 5cm (2 in). It has pale, rounded leaves and bears an abundance of white flowers. It likes a sunny position and a well-drained, slightly alkaline soil.

Thymus azoricus: a neat, mound-forming pine-scented thyme that grows to a height of 10cm (4in) and bears lavender-coloured flowers in early to mid-summer.

Thymus x *citriodorus* 'Aureus': golden lemon thyme is a hardy, evergreen thyme. Its leaves of gold are highly aromatic and it grows to a height of 10–15cm (4–6in) on a well-drained soil and in full sun.

Creeping pennyroyal (*Mentha pulegium* 'Cunningham Mint'): a fragrant, prostrate herb that grows to a height of 10–15cm (4–6in). It has an indefinite spread and thrives in moist soil either in partial shade or sun.

Corsican mint (*Mentha requienii*): smells strongly of peppermint and is an excellent ground cover plant for damp shade. It is the smallest of the mints and forms a carpet of tiny, bright green leaves. It bears small, purple flowers in summer.

BUSHY THYMES AND LAVENDER

Thymus vulgaris 'Silver Posie': has variegated, silver leaves and likes a well-drained soil and plenty of sun. It grows to a height and spread of 25 x 45cm (10 x 18in). Abundant mauve-pink flowers appear in summer.

Thymus fragrantissimus: orange-scented thyme is an attractive, grey-green leaved plant with aromatic, orange/balsam scented foliage and pale pink flowers. It has an upright bushy form and likes full sun and a well-drained, alkaline soil.

Thymus x *citriodorus:* lemon thyme grows to a height and spread of 30 x 60cm (12 x 24in). It is an evergreen dwarf shrub, ideal for scented borders. It can be grown in a container and likes a well-drained soil and full sun.

Lavandula angustifolia 'Nana Alba': this delightful lavender is the smallest of the dwarf lavenders, growing to a height of 25cm (10in) in full sun in a well-drained soil. An evergreen perennial, it has narrow, grey leaves and white flowers.

Golden lemon thyme is a dwarf evergreen

Lavandula angustifolia is an ideal edging for paths

PATHS OF CARPETING HERBS

Herbs of prostrate or semi-prostrate habit will grow into a 'carpet' or can be planted between paving stones. The creeping mints literally cling to the soil, and the creeping thymes are at their best growing over stones.

Carpeting herbs should be planted 20cm (8in) apart and it is good to grow a selection of varieties. A number of species can be grown from seed – the thymes, for example –

A path newly planted with a variety of thymes

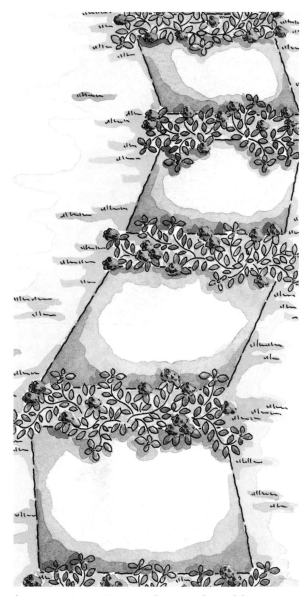

Low-growing mints or thymes planted between paving stones or slabs will soften their edges

and they will be very hardy and long-lasting if the soil is light and well-drained. Bear in mind, though, that the area will have a very sparse appearance during the first year, but this will soon disappear as the plants begin to spread to quickly form a thick carpet.

Stepping stones are useful in lawns, or they can be edged with all manner of low-growing herbs

EDGINGS FOR STEPPING STONES

Position stepping stones across a lawn, or place in gravel or soil. If the stones are positioned in the lawn, place them over the turf, cut round the edges with the tool made for the job, known as a turf moon cutter, then lift each stepping stone and remove the section of turf beneath it. Remove enough soil to ensure that the stone, when repositioned, will be slightly lower than the level of the lawn to make mowing easier. Replace the stone, making sure that it is level.

Remove part of the turf between the stepping stones and plant pennyroyal and a variety of thymes in the spaces. If your stepping stones are placed in gravel, simply remove some of the gravel between each of the stones and plant your herbs in the soil underneath, replacing the gravel when the plants are in place.

PLANTING HERBS BETWEEN PAVING SLABS

STAGE 1: Choose the planting crevices with care, and if the gaps between the paving slabs are mortared, remove the mortar and underneath soil to a depth of 5cm (2in).

STAGE 2: If the crevices are not mortared, then you will have suitable gaps in which to plant. Clear out any weeds, debris and soil and fill the crevices with a loam-based compost.

STAGE 3: Using a small trowel, plant small, rooted herbs in the crevices, adding more

compost as necessary. Alternatively, roots can be eased into small gaps with a knife blade. Firm in gently, using your fingers, to remove any pockets of air.

STAGE 4: Water carefully, and then water regularly until the plants are well established. Do not use powerful jets of water or the plants will be washed away.

As an alternative, seed can be planted in the crevices in a mixture of light compost and horticultural sand. Scatter the herb seed, and then water until established. Try seeding salad burnet in this way.

Creeping thymes in flower are quite breathtakingly beautiful and are seen at their best planted between and cascading over carefully positioned paving slabs

GROWING HERBS ON BANKS

Less hardy, sun-loving herbs can be grown on a sun-facing bank or slope. A group of gently sloping banks can be created down a steep garden, or low banks can be made on a level site. But, whatever kind of site you have, you can create banks which are generally ideal for growing and harvesting herbs: you can even build a bank as part of a raised bed that will also act as a windbreak. Banks are excellent places for growing herbs if space is limited, but any herbs planted on a slope will have to be of the varieties that will withstand some drought, such as horehound (*Marrubium vulgare*) and viper's bugloss (*Echium vulgare*), while those at the foot of the slope need to be moisture-loving species, such as sweet cicely (*Myrrhis odorata*).

The soil will be less crumbly if it is planted and weeded after rain or when you have watered it, although once your herbs have

become established, their roots will spread and make the bank more stable. Creeping thymes are ideal herbs to plant, as are marjoram, calamint, compact savory (*Satureja montana* 'Prostrate White'), as well as spreading herbs such as lady's bedstraw (*Galium verum*) and dwarf comfrey (*Symphytum grandiflorum*). In shady parts, try woodruff (*Galium odoratum*), alpine strawberry (*Fragaria vesca* 'Baron Solemacher'/'Alexandria') and periwinkle (vinca). A bank of poor soil that is in a dry, exposed position can be planted with prostrate herbs – chamomile, creeping mints and thymes are particularly suited to these conditions.

HERB ROCKERIES

Try to site a herb rockery in a sunny corner with a backdrop of trees or plants, if possible. It should be built on a slope, although you can build up a mound on level ground.

A herb rockery will happily accommodate savory, thyme and marjoram and low-growing herbs such as caraway thyme (*Thymus herba-barona*), chives, lemon thyme and golden marjoram. Other herbs to try would be cowslip, rock hyssop, pasque flower (*Pulsatilla vulgaris*), rock rose (*Helianthemum nummularium* 'Amy Baring') and centaury (*Centaurium erythraea*).

STAGE 1: Prepare the site by forking over the soil and removing all weeds and debris.

STAGE 2: To ensure good drainage, lay a 15cm (6in) layer of hardcore and cover with inverted turves to prevent the finer soil from impeding drainage. If turves are unavailable, use polythene sheeting – black refuse sacks are ideal – punching holes in them to allow the water to drain away.

Field poppies are good subjects for a rockery

STAGE 3: Cover with soil to the designated height.

STAGE 4: Place a row of rocks at intervals all around the bottom of the mound, adding more soil as necessary to ensure stability.

STAGE 5: Start building up the rockery by adding more soil and randomly positioning more rocks. Continue to add more soil as each layer of rock is built up, and make sure that the sides slope and that the rockery is built up to a flattish top. Partly bury the rocks and let them slope towards the centre of the mound of soil. Leave spaces between the rocks for herbs.

Thyme and creeping Jenny will thrive in a rockery

A herb rockery is an ideal growing arrangement. If sited in a sunny spot, it will enable you to grow a fine and varied collection of the plants in a very small area

8 GROWING HERBS INDOORS

Herbs are not house plants and accordingly they need to spend their time out of doors. There are, however, many herbs that you can keep indoors, over a period of time, without any permanent harm coming to them. Most of the herbs that grow successfully in pots outside and those which would die down after summer has ended, will continue to grow indoors for most of the year. Herbs grown indoors, however, are not so long-lived and are more likely to become drawn and elongated. Remember that all herbs prefer to be outside in summer.

When choosing herbs for indoor growing, be aware that glass can reduce light by 30–50 per cent, so many of them will fare better on a windowsill, although they will grow well under fluorescent lights at every stage of development. If your plants become drawn and spindly, the chances are that they are not getting enough light. Sun-loving herbs also need at least six hours of sun each day to flourish. Remember to turn your herbs each day for an even amount of sunlight on all sides.

Kitchens are not suitable places to keep herbs, as temperatures fluctuate and there are fumes from cooking. Domestic gas and oil fumes also take their toll. Bathrooms, on the other hand, make good growing rooms, as do conservatories, sunny porches or greenhouses.

A selection of herbs, growing in pots on a well-lit windowsill

HERBS FOR GROWING INDOORS

Scented-leaf geraniums

These are ideal plants for the blind or partially sighted and will flourish quite happily indoors. They are quite different from other geraniums because the scented-leaf varieties are normally cultivated for their perfume, which is released when the leaves are gently brushed. The flowers, however, are somewhat insignificant. Scented-leaf geraniums can grow to quite gigantic proportions if left untrained, so severe pruning will be necessary. There are many species of these geraniums, with a vast choice of perfumes. Obviously they will not attain the same height as they would in the garden, but they will give great pleasure if they are repotted in fresh compost every year and moved to a larger pot when necessary.

Rosemary

Rarely grows to over 1m (39in) in a container. It flourishes in a bright position, but needs a cooler temperature of around 15°C (60°F) if it is to produce flowers. It is an ideal plant for the conservatory.

Sages

Also make excellent conservatory plants. Try growing pineapple sage (*Salvia elegans* 'Scarlet Pineapple'), with its long, pointed leaves and bright scarlet flowers, 4cm (1¼in) in length. Common sage will also grow well indoors, as will the coloured leaved varieties: 'Icterina', with its gold, variegated leaves; 'Purpurascens', with its dark purple leaves; or 'Tricolor', with its irregularly slashed, creamy-white foliage. The plants, which can be kept in any room in the house, should be clipped back to a manageable size and shape.

Scented-leaf geraniums will flourish indoors

Pelargonium x *citrosum* (*P. crispum* hybrid), *P. crispum* 'Variegatum' and 'Prince Rupert' geranium all have lemon-scented foliage, the latter having greyish leaves, 2–2.5cm (¾–1in) wide, with crisped or curled edges. Peppermint-scented geranium (*P. tomentosum*) is a shrubby, sprawling example with particularly erect stems to 1m (39in) in length. Its peppermint-scented leaves are triangular and grow to 12.5cm (5in) across.

Sage 'Icterina' has golden, variegated leaves

Purple sage will grow well in a conservatory

Pot marigolds require a cool position

Pot marigold

A plant to brighten up the dullest corner with its tiny-petalled, round, orange flower heads. It is a plant that doesn't like heat, so it's important to find a cool spot for it. Pinch out the top shoot and, if you want a short, sturdy plant for container growing, make sure it gets plenty of sunlight and keep the soil moist. Marigolds are in flower for most of the year if dead headed regularly.

Lemon verbena

Aloysia triphylla is a deciduous shrub with pointed, lemon-scented leaves and sprays of mauve flowers in summer that will grow to 1.5m (5ft) in a temperate climate. Grow the herb out of doors in a pot small enough to take indoors for winter. A conservatory is an ideal place to keep it, or on the windowsill of a sun room. Don't be tempted to place it in a warm room as it will wilt rapidly and fail to thrive. Lemon verbena, like bay, prefers filtered sun and a rich soil.

Purple-leaved basil

Ocimum basilicum 'Purple Ruffles' or 'Dark Opal' is an annual that will grow indoors, usually to a height of 45–60cm (18–24in). Grow in a free-draining compost, and don't allow it to become waterlogged.

Bay

Small specimens of sweet bay (*Laurus nobilis*) can also be grown in pots and are best cultivated from cuttings taken in summer or bought as pot plants. If your bay is small, other herbs can be planted with it: try thyme, winter savory or marjoram.

Bay is often grown in a pot, for decoration

Myrtle is valuable for its foliage, flowers and fruits

Myrtle

Myrtus communis can be grown indoors where the height and spread can be confined to 60–90cm (2–3ft). The plant, which has aromatic foliage, lovely flowers and, usually, decorative fruits, is ideal for a cold conservatory.

Roses

Young scented roses, of standard or bush varieties, will also flourish indoors in pots. Prune the bushes in mid-winter by removing the weak shoots and cutting back the other stems to just above the fourth strong bud above the base. When you bring them indoors increase the temperature slowly from around 5°C (41°F) at night, to 8°C (46°F) by day in mid-winter, to about 13°C (55°F) at night and 18°C (64°F) by day in late spring. Make sure that you place them in a well-lit spot. Keep the compost moist and spray the foliage to maintain humidity. When buds start to form, feed them with a liquid

fertilizer every seven to ten days. Once the plants have stopped flowering move them out of doors. Try the hybrid tea 'Ena Harkness' with its red blooms, or the floribunda 'Fleur Cowles' with its pink, scented flowers.

Curry plant and eucalyptus

Both of these are also suitable for indoor cultivation. Try *Eucalyptus citriodora*, with its attractive leaves which give off a strong lemon scent when rubbed.

Jasmine

The fragrant *Jasminum polyanthum* bears fragrant, white flowers in early spring and can be trained around canes. It can be grown in a cool conservatory, but it is a vigorous grower that needs to be kept under control by drastic pruning.

Roses grown indoors must have plenty of light

HOW TO PLANT HERBS FOR GROWING INDOORS

When planting herbs indoors, remember that with central heating the plants will require plenty of fresh air and adequate watering. Herbs with large, soft leaves in active growth or in small pots will need frequent watering, but do not over-water. Root rot fungus will flourish in waterlogged soil and important air pockets in the soil can be eliminated. The occasional soak, though, is much appreciated.

All annuals should be started from seed and perennials from cuttings. Sow annual and biennial herb seed in late summer in 7.5cm (3in) pots to start them off. Bring them indoors, moving them on to larger pots as they grow.

Growing herbs in seed trays

You can grow from seed either by buying it in packets, or by harvesting your own. Annuals and biennials such as dill, borage, summer savory and chervil will give quick results, although others will be slow to raise.

Basil seedlings can be grown in a seed tray

Sow seed indoors by sprinkling it on a tray of compost, following the instructions on the packet. Usually, the seed should be sown 6–12mm (¼–½in) deep. Use a suitable growing medium, such as John Innes seed mixture, and make sure that it is level and slightly firmed. Water lightly and place the tray in a plastic freezer bag. Inflate the bag by blowing into it and tie the top, keeping the tray away from direct sunlight. Once the seedlings germinate – germination time will vary according to the herb – remove the bag and, when they are large enough to handle, transplant them into another pot or tray to give them more room.

If you only need a few specimens of each herb, plant the seed in pots. Sow thickly because clumps of seedlings are much easier to transplant. Don't let the seedlings get burned by strong sunlight, and once true leaves appear above the seed leaves, transplant clumps of five or six seedlings into small pots. Place on a windowsill to provide early pickings.

An easy way of raising herbs from seed is to buy the special packs of seed and compost designed to help germination. These packs are made up of peat pots, each one containing a suitable growing medium and one species of herb. Once planted, the pots are covered with the transparent, plastic dome provided. This acts like a miniature greenhouse and the seed soon begins to germinate. Herb seed is most at risk when it just begins to germinate, so it is vital that the soil is kept moist. If the compost dries out the seed will not germinate and if too much water is applied to the seedlings before their roots develop, they will collapse and die. Try using a mist spray to keep the soil just moist.

Thin out the seedlings when they appear and transfer the peat pot into a plant pot filled with compost. You can then leave the roots of the herbs to grow through the peat pots into the compost and continue growing to their full size.

Small pieces of the roots of herbs such as mint, as well as clumps of chives, can be lifted in late summer and planted up in pots. Mint can be left outside until after the first frost. Herbs such as tarragon and lemon balm should be lifted by mid-autumn, potted up and left to establish in a shady corner for about a month. As they need time to acclimatize before being brought indoors, leave them outside during the day and bring them in at night.

In late summer/early autumn, cut back herbs intended for indoors to around 15cm (6in) high and lift enough of the herb to fill a 10–15cm (4–6in) pot filled with a multi-purpose compost.

It is a good idea to plant up three pots of any herb that you use frequently. The first plant should be cut back to around 2.5cm (1in) in late summer/early autumn, and the second plant harvested for the next four weeks, after which time any remaining shoots should be cut back. Harvest the third plant for the following month, after which it too should be cut right back, by which time the first plant will be ready to use again. Thus, you will have one plant in use, a new one ready to use, and one recovering. The number of varieties of herbs you will be able to cultivate in this way will depend upon the space available.

Filling a pot

The health and vigour of the plants depend largely on the rooting medium, and the best compost for pot plants is one that is well aerated, holds moisture, contains plenty of nutrients and is free-draining.

STAGE 1: Place a layer of drainage material such as crocks at the bottom of the pot.

STAGE 2: Add about 5cm (2in) of horticultural sand – to stop the compost from clogging – and then fill the pot two-thirds full with a soil-less compost.

STAGE 3: Make a hole in the middle of the compost, set the herb into it, settling the compost around its roots.

STAGE 4: Continue to fill with compost to 2.5cm (1in) below the rim of the pot.

STAGE 5: Water well with a fine spray to settle in the plant and then stand the pot in a saucer of gravel. This will allow for the drainage of excess water and keep the atmosphere around the plant humid.

STAGE 6: Feed your plant with a liquid fertilizer at the intervals recommended in the manufacturer's instructions.

Mint can be potted up and taken indoors

Aftercare

After planting, water very sparingly and only when the compost seems to be drying out. Plants that are kept too wet are likely to rot. Herbs grow best at a minimum temperature of 15°C (60°F) and they don't like sudden draughts or changes in temperature, but the room should be ventilated when the weather permits. Good light is also important – use shading to prevent the foliage from burning if it is particularly sunny. Be vigilant regarding insect pests such as aphids and carrot fly. Newly potted herbs will not require feeding for at least a month because of the nutrients already present in the new compost. Most herbs flourish better in groups; they are easier to water and they respond well to the mini-climate that grouping creates. Mist spray during summer to maintain good humidity.

THE POT-BOUND PLANT

It is important to recognize when a plant is pot bound. You will find that it is growing very slowly, even in good light and warmth with regular watering and feeding and good air circulation. Roots may be growing through the drainage holes. To make sure, remove the plant from its container. If the roots are thickly matted and twine around the pot, then your plant is ready to be potted-on.

Potting-on

Healthy plants soon outgrow their pots and need to be potted-on regularly if they are to grow and keep their shape. Make sure that

Allow the pot to drain. Afterwards water very sparingly: only when the compost is drying out

A herb removed from its pot. Its roots are thickly matted and it is ready to be potted-on

you move gradually up the pot sizes – round pots are listed by a number which represents their diameter and their approximate height – as placing a plant in a pot that is too big will encourage a weak root system and the plant will look out of proportion with its pot. Tap-rooted herbs such as borage, dill, chervil and parsley do best in deep pots.

STAGE 1: The new pot should allow at least 2.5cm (1in) of extra space around the plant that is to be potted on. Place drainage material (such as crocks or gravel) and a layer of compost in the bottom.

STAGE 2: Make sure the herb you are potting-on is moist and remove it from its pot by inverting the pot across your upturned hand with the plant hanging between your fingers. To loosen the pot, tap the rim against a hard surface. Lift the pot off the plant.

STAGE 3: Tease out the roots of the herb and sit it on the compost.

STAGE 4: Fill in the sides of the pot with more compost, firming with your fingers. When finished, the rootball should be covered with about 1cm (½in) of compost.

STAGE 5: Water well with a fine spray and leave to drain.

Potting-on *v*. repotting

Potting-on differs from repotting in that when you repot, you are keeping the plant in the same sized container and just giving it a change of compost.

Repotting is the method used for plants that are not required to grow much bigger, and that have been in the same growing medium for several years.

The bigger pot is part-filled with compost, the herb centred in it, and the remaining space filled

PRUNING

Herbs grown indoors are pruned in much the same way as outdoor ones. Scented-leaf geraniums, for example, make vigorous annual growth and should be cut back severely just as growth is about to start, otherwise you will be left with untidy, straggly plants. To encourage bushy growth and flowers, your herbs will need to be 'stopped' from time to time. This means that the growing tip or shoot should be removed – but only when the plant is actively growing. Left to their own devices some herbs will continue growing until they reach maximum size, which could result in limited flowering and bare stems appearing at the base of the plant. Overcrowding such as this can also encourage disease.

INDOOR HANGING BASKETS

Moss gives the most natural look to the baskets when used as a liner, and using soil-less composts like peat and coir means that the hanging baskets are considerably lighter, but that they will need watering more often. Plant the taller growing herbs in the top of the basket, with the low-growing and trailing ones around the sides. Regular harvesting will keep the baskets neat.

Parsley is easily grown in an indoor hanging basket

Herbs for indoor hanging baskets

Aromatic thymes make excellent basket fillers. Plant your basket with lemon thyme (*Thymus* x *citriodorus* 'Goldstream'), and the useful kitchen thyme, caraway thyme (*Thymus herba–barona*).

Chives (*Allium schoenoprasum*) make a neat and colourful addition to a hanging basket. They have tubular, grass-like leaves to 10–25cm (4–10in) and round heads of purple flowers from early to mid-summer. They should never be allowed to dry out and are greedy feeders.

Basil (ocimum): the purple leaves of *Ocimum basilicum* var. *aurauascens* contrast well with the different greens of other herbs. There are many different varieties of basil to try, such as the lemon-scented *O. basilicum* var. *citriodorum* with its green leaves and white flowers.

Sages (salvia): plant rooted cuttings of sage in your basket, trimming them to shape as they grow. There are many types of sage – try purple sage (*Salvia officinalis* 'Purpurascens Group'), for instance, or the wonderful-smelling pineapple sage (*Salvia elegans* 'Scarlet Pineapple').

Chervil (*Anthriscus cerefolium*) with its lacy leaves, is suitable for over-wintering in a hanging basket. Remove its flowering stems to promote maximum leaf growth.

Nasturtium (*Tropaeolum majus*) 'Double Gleam Mixed' and 'Whirlybird Series' range from scarlet and orange, to yellow and cream. You could also try 'Alaska Mixed' with its variegated foliage.

Mints (mentha): there are many different varieties of mint. Try growing ginger mint (*Mentha* x *gracilis* 'Variegata') with its bright green and yellow variegated leaves, spicy scent and shorter growing habit. Contain each root in a polythene bag filled with compost, but don't forget to cut drainage holes in the bottom of the bag.

Feverfew (*Tanacetum parthenium* formerly *Chrysanthemum*) grows to a height of 45cm (18in) and can be over-wintered indoors. The leaves are yellowy-green, segmented and aromatic when crushed.

Salad burnet (*Sanguisorba minor*) low-growing and decorative, and holds its cucumber-scented leaves throughout the winter. When the leaves become coarse, cut back the whole plant.

Pot marigold (*Calendula officinalis*): a decorative plant with its splashes of orange flowers. Sowing seed in late summer will provide plants which will over-winter and flower early the following year.

Parsley (*Petroselinum crispum*): easy to grow in a variety of ways, from planting it in a small strawberry pot or a 'crocus' pot, which has pockets set all over the surface, to growing it in a hanging basket, where it will grow really well.

Summer savory (*Satureja hortensis*): with its widely branched stem and long, pointed, dark green leaves, it is a good subject for a hanging basket. It has whorls of lilac, white or purple flowers in summer. It is sensitive to cold and needs a sunny position.

Nasturtium 'Alaska' grows well in a basket indoors

Some herb combinations

- A combination of basil, summer savory and marjoram looks attractive.
- Plant chives, parsley and variegated mints together.
- Nasturtiums look splendid with the bright green leaves of parsley.

Curled sweet basil has a wonderful flavour

INDOOR HERBS FOR THE KITCHEN

It is worth trying to grow a continuous supply of culinary herbs because fresh herbs always have a better flavour than dried ones. Some varieties can be potted up in autumn or seed can be sown in late summer. They can be kept in a warm greenhouse or conservatory, where they will receive more light. Fennel and tarragon can be over-wintered in pots indoors, and small pieces of the roots of established herbs such as mint, chives and fennel can be lifted in late summer and potted up.

Herbs for the kitchen

Summer savory (*Satureja hortensis*): dig out of the garden in late summer, pot it up and take indoors. Summer savory grows to a height of 10–38cm (4–15in), and its leaves have a sharp, spicy flavour.

Basil (*ocimum*): needs warmth and bright light. Sow the seed in late summer and place on a sunny windowsill. Water sparingly as the days get shorter. The seedlings will produce fresh growth for many months. Bush basil (*Ocimum basilicum* var. *minimum*) grows to about 15cm (6in), while sweet basil (*Ocimum basilicum*) can grow to 60cm (24in). An Italian strain, *Ocimum basilicum* 'Genovese', can be grown for pesto, and purple-leaved basil (*Ocimum basilicum* var. *aurauascens*) has a very strong flavour.

Chives (*Allium schoenoprasum*): lift a clump of chives and split into smaller pieces before potting up and bringing indoors. Trim back the foliage to encourage fresh shoots to develop. When potted, give a good watering to settle them in, but water very sparingly afterwards. They will grow strongly from the middle of autumn to mid-spring.

Chervil (*Anthriscus cerefolium*): grown for its bright green, feathery leaves and aniseed flavour. When growing indoors, it should be given light shade and humidity. The plant will grow to a height of 30–45cm (12–18in).

Sweet marjoram (*Origanum majorana*): grown as a half-hardy annual, will reach a height of 30cm (12in). A winter supply can be provided by potting up established plants in sandy soil in late summer.

PLANTING AN INDOOR HERB VEGETABLE RACK

You will need:
A three-tier vegetable rack
Polythene sheeting
Gravel
Compost
Selection of herbs

STAGE 4: Water using a small watering can, and allow to settle.

STAGE 1: Line each basket at the bottom and sides with pieces of polythene. Place a layer of gravel or pebbles over the polythene for drainage.

STAGE 2: Fill each basket with a good quality potting compost.

STAGE 3: Plant the herbs (see next page), making wells in the compost to accommodate them. Firm in well, but gently so that the herbs are not damaged.

STAGE 5: Position the vegetable rack in a well-lit, draught-free spot.

Try to ensure that the rack gets as much sunlight as possible during the day. Feed the herbs with a liquid fertilizer at the intervals recommended on the packet.

Maintenance

Water when necessary, but don't allow the baskets to become waterlogged. Feed the herbs every two weeks with a liquid feed. Spray them occasionally to ensure a good level of humidity. Trim and harvest regularly to keep the plants under control and in good, neat shape.

Planting suggestions for herb racks

Top tier
Chervil (*Anthriscus cerefolium*)
Lemon balm (*Melissa officinalis*)
Nasturtium (*Tropaeolum majus* 'Alaska')
Pot marjoram (*Origanum onites*)
Sage (salvia)
Spearmint (*Mentha spicata*)
Summer savory (*Satureja hortensis*)
Sweet basil (*Ocimum basilicum*)

Middle tier
Basil minette (*Ocimum basilicum* 'Minette')
Bay (*Laurus nobilis*) (small rooted cutting)
Borage (*Borago officinalis*)
English lavender (*Lavandula angustifolia*)
Feverfew (*Tanacetum parthenium* formerly
    Chrysanthemum)
Rosemary (*Rosmarinus officinalis*)
Winter savory (*Satureja montana*)

Bottom tier
Bush basil (*Ocimum basilicum* var. *minimum*)
Chives (*Allium schoenoprasum*)
Curry plant (*Helichrysum italicum* syn.
    H. angustifolium)
Garlic chives (*Allium tuberosum*)
Parsley (*Petroselinum crispum*)
Thyme (*Thymus vulgaris*)
Tricolour sage (*Salvia officinalis* var. *tricolor*)

GROWING HERBS ON WINDOWSILLS

Most herbs will grow well on a sunny windowsill at a temperature of between 13–18°C (55–65°F). They will, however, have a milder fragrance than when grown outside. You can buy them ready potted and repot them if necessary and then leave them outside for a couple of weeks before bringing them indoors. They can then be placed on a windowsill, either in a saucer of gravel or on a plastic lined tray. Remember to water them once the top of the soil is dry and to feed them every 10 to 14 days. You can plant up a selection of herbs together in a light, plastic trough, provided that they grow at roughly the same rate.

Kitchen windowsills

Herbs such as parsley, mint and chives are the toughest herbs, and the only ones that will tolerate the temperature fluctuations, chilling draughts and temporary increase in humidity that can be found on a kitchen windowsill. Mint will flourish if planted in a

Lemon balm, pot marjoram and lemon verbena on a windowsill

separate, large container, and allowed to stand in a saucer or drip tray of water. Fill the bottom third of the pot with crocks or gravel. This ensures that any surplus water is held in this open layer, so that the soil does not become waterlogged and remains aerated. Chives need less sun but, when grown in a pot, they are prone to greenfly invasion. If this happens, douse the plant well with soapy water, which should solve the problem.

Other windowsills

Thyme, marjoram, sage and basil will all flourish on a windowsill with a more stable environment. Herbs prefer a windowsill that is draught-free and brightly lit, sunny and with a temperature of around 10–16°C (50–60°F). A south- or south-west-facing windowsill is best during winter. Annuals such as basil, summer savory and sweet marjoram will last longer under such conditions; mint, sage, chives, thyme, parsley and fennel will flourish; and even cuttings of rosemary planted up will thrive. The compost should be kept moist, initially, but it should remain almost dry during late autumn and winter when growth slows down and light levels become less. Thyme and sage should be placed nearest to the window to protect shade-loving herbs such as mint, chervil and variegated lemon balm from the sun.

Rosemary, sage and bay will all do well in larger pots, while chives, chervil, thyme and savory are ideal for smaller containers. Thyme, sage, marjoram, scented-leaf geraniums and dwarf lavenders such as *Lavandula angustifolia* 'Nana Alba' enjoy direct sun. Dill, savory and chives like full sun, but they prefer a lower temperature. Other herbs which prefer a bright situation and a cooler temperature – 15°C (60°F) – are rosemary, salad burnet, coriander and parsley.

Sweet basil is an ideal candidate for a windowsill

Maintenance

Pots of herbs grown on indoor windowsills are more vulnerable than plants in the open ground and therefore need more care. Make sure all containers are adequately drained. Indoor herbs need a drip tray or saucer where excess water can collect. Spray the plants to keep them moist. If air, light, water and nutrients are supplied in adequate amounts, the herbs will flourish.

9 HARVESTING AND PRESERVING HERBS

Herbs hanging to dry on a kitchen dresser

While herbs have great ornamental value, they are really intended for use. All but the evergreens, however, can only be freshly picked for a limited period of the year – late spring to early autumn usually – so they need to be preserved if they are to be used all year round. The best time to harvest varies from plant to plant. Careless harvesting and storing will spoil all the hard work put into growing the plants, so make sure you know which parts to pick: usually the leaves and stems, but sometimes the seeds, flowers or roots.

Herbs can be harvested when they are well established, with enough growth not to be adversely affected. Usually the tips of the stems are harvested to encourage the plant to make more growth. The aim is to preserve all of the herb's volatile oil, which gives it its flavour, and as much natural colour as possible. The essential oils, which are concentrated in the leaves, are not as strong during winter, so don't over-pick outside the growing season because the herb will not be renewing itself.

SELECTING HERBS FOR HARVESTING

Evergreen herbs, such as sage, thyme, rosemary and winter savory can be picked throughout the year (although winter savory should be given the chance to harden off before winter comes), and the fresh leaves of all herbs can be picked for immediate use throughout the growing season.

Harvest only one species of herb at a time. Plants growing under optimum conditions can be harvested in mid-summer and again in autumn. The shrubby sages, the thymes and tarragon will usually bear two crops. Much depends upon the weather, and herbs will always be at their best following a dry summer. Whatever the climate, however, there will be a time when each herb will have reached full maturity and begin to die back. Obviously, the plant must be harvested before this happens.

If gathering herbs from the wild, make sure that your plant identification is correct as some herbs are poisonous. If you are not absolutely certain, leave well alone. You also need to be sure that the herbs you collect are not contaminated in any way by pollutants such as pesticides or herbicides or, if near a road, by lead from the atmosphere.

Remember that most countries have protected species, so check that you are within the law before picking.

WHEN, WHAT AND HOW OF HARVESTING

Always harvest on a dry day. If herbs are cut when wet, not only are they difficult to handle, but mildew may set in before they can be preserved and the crop will be lost. Pick when the plants are at their most potent: in the morning when they are just open and after the dew has dried, but before the heat of the sun. Never harvest more herbs than you can deal with quickly. If you cannot begin the preserving process straight away, strip off the lower leaves and place the stems in a jug of cold water in a cool, dark place. Herbs that are left lying around quickly lose their flavour.

A trug containing freshly harvested herbs, where they will not sweat, or get crushed or bruised

A variety of air-dried herbs, ready to be stored in air-tight containers

Harvesting leaves and stems

Use a sharp knife to cut the stems of small-leaved herbs; larger leaves can be picked by hand. Try to handle as little as possible to avoid bruising, and remove any browned or damaged leaves. Harvest the leaves just before the plant comes into flower, otherwise the flavour of the leaves will not be as good. Cut flowers for preservation just as they become fully open.

Cut back perennial herbs by about one-third and annuals to the bottom leaves. Don't cut all the plant's growth if you want fresh leaves later in the season. Herbs tend to heat up quickly, so don't place them in a bag or they will begin to sweat and get crushed and bruised. Lay them on a trug or wooden tray. If the leaves are muddy or dusty wash them

gently and then shake them to remove as much moisture as possible. Work quickly so that the scents and flavours are preserved.

Upright thymes can be bunched together, held with one hand, and then cut with a sharp knife about 7.5cm (3in) from the base. Cut angelica stems in early summer for candying.

Harvesting flowers

Cut flowers for preservation just as they become fully open. Cut lavender when in full bloom, and also lady's mantle (*Alchemilla mollis*), otherwise the flowers could fall apart when fully dry. This plant peaks in early summer. Flowers do not improve in colour once they are picked, and they must be picked at the correct time if they are not to shrivel or drop.

Harvesting seeds

Caraway, coriander, dill, fennel and lovage should be harvested for their seed. Seed should be gathered when the seed heads turn brown. Tap the seed heads on a daily basis, and, if the seeds begin to fall, the herb is ready to be gathered. Don't allow the seeds to fall and scatter, and don't leave them in the wet or they will become mouldy.

Harvesting roots and bulbs

Harvest roots in autumn when the tops of the plants are beginning to wither and die down. Scrub the roots as soon as they are lifted, remove fibrous parts, and cut into small pieces before drying.

DRYING HERBS

The aim of drying herbs is to change them as little as possible while removing the water content. Herbs are about 70 per cent water, and the secret is to remove that water as quickly as possible without losing any of the volatile oils. Leaves are going to lose about 75 per cent of the water in them; roots a little less. By drying herbs, you are, in effect, dehydrating them to a point at which mould and bacteria can no longer develop.

A lot of herbs will keep their flavour when dried; some flavours will even improve, by becoming more concentrated than that of fresh herbs. Avoid washing the leaves, unless absolutely necessary, keep them out of the sunlight, and dry them in the shortest time possible. Treat flowers in exactly the same way. If flowers are dried correctly, they will keep their colour, the leaves and stems will remain green, and there will be no problem with mildew. Some of the best flowers to dry for later use are borage, chamomile, elder, honeysuckle, marigold petals, meadowsweet, rose petals and violets.

Coriander seeds harvested, ready for air drying

Always dry herbs in the dark. If they are dried in the light, natural or otherwise, they will lose both quality and colour as the volatile oils evaporate in the heat. They also need a good circulation of air around them and good ventilation to carry away the humidity that drying plants create. Although the temperature at which to dry varies according to the requirements of individual herbs, it should remain constant. A temperature of between 24–26°C (75–80°F) is reasonable, but it should be a little higher for the first 24 hours if possible.

Herbs are dry when they are brittle enough to snap and crackle when pressed. Fully dried leaves will part from the stems and they will crumble, not fall into dust. They will also have a lovely aromatic smell, and will keep for about nine months to a year, although lovage, mint and marjoram will keep for longer. Bear in mind, though, that if they are kept too long, they will lose their flavour, colour and scent.

Air drying

Air drying is the traditional way of preserving herbs. It relies on air to dry out the moisture in the plants.

Stems and leaves

Remove damaged leaves and woody stems from the cut herbs and tie the stems with twine in small bundles – about 10–12 stems to a bunch. Tie them loosely with a slip knot so that the knot can be tightened as the stems shrink. Don't pack the leaves too tightly and don't mix the different species. Strip off any lower leaves that could get caught up in the twine.

Rig up a line of string or twine in a warm, dry, airy place away from direct sunlight. Hang the herbs upside down so that air can circulate around them, using a clothes peg or paperclip to secure them to the line. Herbs such as mint, rosemary, sage, bay, savory and thyme can be dried in this way.

Excluding humidity is also very important, so don't use anywhere that is likely to become damp: steamy kitchens and bathrooms, for example. On a warm, dry day, herbs can be left outside suspended from a clothes airer, away from direct sunlight.

Alternatively, trays can be made from pieces of muslin stretched over wooden frames and then placed on supports to allow air to circulate underneath. Herbs can also be spread on trays with perforations that will allow the air to circulate, or on slatted shelves. Turn them for several weeks until quite dry. You could also use shallow boxes lined with paper, again turning frequently. Herbs can also be dried in an airy, well-ventilated garden shed, an attic or even a cupboard under the stairs. If you use a

A line of herbs being air dried in a warm, dry garden shed, away from direct sunlight

cupboard, leave the door open slightly to allow dampness to escape as the herbs are drying.

The drying period of each herb will vary. Seven to ten days is a good average, but this will depend upon the thickness of the leaves. Never allow herbs to dry until the leaves collapse on contact.

Low-growing herbs such as summer savory, woodruff and centaury should be dried whole with their stems. Strip the leaves from their stems on large herbs such as sweet cicely and lovage before drying, and dry the thick, fleshy leaves of herbs such as comfrey, sage and coltsfoot individually.

Flowers and petals

Hang flowers and petals in small amounts in netting bags – the ones that you get from supermarkets in which vegetables and fruit are sold. They come in different mesh sizes. Never fill the bags completely, and give each bag a shake occasionally. Alternatively, arrange flower heads still on their stems at varying heights so that the air can circulate more easily around them.

Alternatively you can place petals and small flowers between sheets of newspaper to dry, or spread them out on muslin-covered frames (see page 148).

The length of time it takes for a flower to dry will depend upon its moisture content and the moisture in the atmosphere. When the flower stem is dry and rigid, the flower is ready for storage. Flower petals will feel dry and 'papery'.

Suitable flowers for air drying include fennel, yarrow, dill, chives, feverfew, cornflowers, chamomile, lady's mantle, rosebuds, lavender and marigolds.

When cutting lavender, lay the stems in a flat basket with all the flower heads together. This will make bunching easier. Never leave

Chamomile flowers can be air dried in a net bag

cut lavender in bundles on a table because the moist heat that is generated will spoil the perfume. When air drying lavender, place a dust sheet underneath the bunches to catch any falling flowers.

Seed heads

Cut the stems of seed heads of herbs such as fennel, dill, coriander, cumin and caraway, tie in bunches and hang upside down with the seed heads suspended in paper bags. When dry, the seeds will 'crack' when touched, and should crumble between the finger nails. Remove them from the paper bags and store.

Roots

Spread sliced or cut pieces of root on drying trays and leave in a warm, dark place, such as an airing cupboard, until they become hard and brittle.

Bunches of lavender tied, labelled and ready to dry

Oven drying

Herbs can be dried in the oven, but be careful to do this gently, as too much heat will dry out the essential oils, thus removing the scent or flavour.

Bunch and tie the herbs and then string them from the oven racks or spread them out on foil on the racks themselves. Set the oven at the lowest setting of 110°C/225°F/gas mark ¼. Leave the door open. Turn them frequently to allow moisture to escape. Depending on the herb and the season, drying can take several hours.

You should never place plant material in a gas oven that is lit because the volatile oils in the herbs can cause a fire hazard. A gas oven should always be turned off before plant material is placed in it, with the door left ajar.

The leaves of tough-stemmed herbs such as bay should be removed before they are placed in the oven. These can be individually positioned on the racks to dry. Large sage leaves can also be dried individually, while the smaller ones can be bunched. The leaves of rosemary and thyme can be dried in bunches. Roots of herbs such as horseradish (*Armoracia rusticana*), angelica (*Angelica archangelica*) and marsh mallow (*Althaea officinalis*) can also be dried in an oven.

Microwave drying

Microwave drying speeds up the process of drying without affecting the flavour of the herbs, and is successful because of the short processing time involved. It is, however, difficult to dry large quantities of plant material in this way, as only limited amounts can be dried at one time.

Place small bunches of herbs or individual fleshy leaves on kitchen paper in a single layer in the microwave, making sure that no two pieces are touching, and process on a low power for about 2–3 minutes. The timing will depend upon the moisture content and the thickness of the leaves, so drying can take longer.

Leaves of herbs such as rosemary, sage and lavender microwave well, as do the flower clusters of chamomile, lady's mantle, tansy, yarrow and marjoram. When using the microwave, check your plant material every 30 or 40 seconds once it is almost ready. Remove leaves and flowers as soon as they are crisp and papery. Don't leave them for even a few seconds too long or they will become too brittle. Remember that microwaves vary in power, so it will be necessary to experiment with drying times. When drying aromatic herbs, keep a close eye on them because the volatile oils could vaporize and catch fire.

Microwaving sage leaves

STAGE 1: Select about 10–12 leaves of uniform size.

STAGE 2: Place the leaves on a piece of kitchen paper, trimming it to size if necessary, and making sure that the leaves don't touch.

STAGE 3: Microwave on 450W for 4 minutes 30 seconds – this timing will depend on the size of the leaves – turning the leaves half-way through the process.

STAGE 4: Keep a close eye on the leaves, stopping the microwave from time to time to check them.

STAGE 5: When ready, remove the leaves from the oven and test for dryness and crispness.

STAGE 6: Store the dried leaves in an airtight container until ready to use.

Ten golden rules for harvesting and drying

1 Always harvest herbs in the morning once the dew has dried and before the heat of the sun has had chance to evaporate the volatile oils.

2 Never pick herbs on a wet day or after rain when they will still be damp.

3 Only harvest herbs that are established, in prime condition, and that are at their most potent. Never over-pick.

4 Use a sharp knife to avoid the possibility of bruising, and avoid handling as much as possible.

5 Only harvest the amount of herbs you are able to deal with quickly. Any that can't be dealt with immediately should be placed in water in a cool, shady spot.

6 Never place cut herbs in a plastic bag. They will sweat and get bruised.

7 Separate herbs into small bunches. Keep each species and variety separate to avoid cross-flavouring. Label and date each batch.

8 Never select herbs that have damaged leaves or flowers or that are suffering from any disease or pest infestation.

9 Dry all herbs in the shortest time possible, with a moderate heat, good air circulation and adequate ventilation.

10 Dry all plant material in a dark place.

Storing dried herbs

Once dried, all herbs should be stored as quickly as possible so that they don't re-absorb any moisture from the atmosphere. If this happens, they will deteriorate and become musty. Strip the leaves from the stems and store whole, crumbling just before use. Place them in air-tight containers in a cool, dark place. Dark glass jars with a screw top are preferable to plastic ones which will make the dried material sweat. If you notice moisture on the inside of the containers, the herbs are not completely dry. Take them out, lay them out on paper, and allow them further drying time.

Sage, rosemary and thyme can be left on their stalks. Bay leaves should be left whole, and all seeds and flowers placed in air-tight containers. Check regularly for any mould and throw the herbs away if any is found. Always label and date any containers you use so that you know their age exactly.

Air-dried marigolds, ready for storage. The petals are removed and stored in an air-tight jar

DECORATIVE USES FOR HERBS

Herbs can be kept supple by preserving them in a solution of glycerine. This changes the colour of the foliage, gives it added sheen and ensures that it lasts indefinitely. The stems in the solution take up the mixture and carry it to all parts of the plant: you can actually see the glycerine working its way up the leaf veins and spreading over the whole leaf. The water gradually evaporates and the plant cells retain the glycerine. Different varieties of leaves turn different colours: the pattern of the fleshy leaves of clary and nasturtium, for example, becoming more pronounced, while those of bay and rosemary become slightly darker and retain their perfume.

You will need:
Bottle of glycerine
Water: hot, but not boiling
Bottle for mixing the solution
Large jar or vase
Cotton wool
Dry containers: vases, jars
Hammer
Herbs

STAGE 1: Prepare the herbs by stripping off any low-growing leaves and crushing the ends of any woody stems, such as those of sage and bay, with a hammer.

STAGE 2: Mix one part glycerine with two parts very hot water in a bottle. Screw on the top and shake thoroughly. Pour the solution into a container, such as a large jar or vase, to a depth of about 5cm (2in).

STAGE 3: Completely submerge the stem ends of the herbs in the glycerine and water and leave the container in a dry place away from strong light for at least three days. The length of time the process takes will vary from herb to herb and larger pieces, such as branches of bay or rosemary, may take longer. Don't use branches that are too tall and be sure to remove any damaged leaves.

STAGE 4: Dip a piece of cotton wool into the glycerine solution and coat any thick leaves with it. This will prevent the leaves from curling and the process can be repeated at regular intervals. Replenish the glycerine solution if necessary.

STAGE 5: Remove the stems from the solution as soon as the leaves have changed colour and stopped taking in liquid. The material should now be soft, supple and shiny.

STAGE 6: Wash and dry the stems and store upright in dry containers. The glycerine solution should not be discarded as it can be used again. Store it in a covered bottle and reheat before use.

NB: Herbs preserved in this way are used solely in decorative arrangements. They should never be eaten or used in cooking.

Soft, supple herbs, after soaking in glycerine

STORING IN THE REFRIGERATOR

First wash the herbs and dry them gently on kitchen paper, handling them carefully so that they don't bruise. Place them in a plastic bag and store them in the refrigerator, but not near the freezer compartment. They will also keep for several days if placed in a covered container.

FREEZING

Freezing is an ideal method of preserving herbs with a delicate flavour and foliage and which do not dry successfully: chervil, salad burnet and sweet cicely, for example. Once harvested, freeze the herbs as quickly as possible in small batches. Herb sprigs can be frozen in small, plastic freezer bags or placed in small plastic containers – this way they tend to be less mushy when defrosted. Make sure that the containers are airtight to prevent other frozen foods from becoming tainted by the herbs' aroma. Label and date all containers.

Preparing sprigs of parsley for freezing

Freezing is a popular method of preserving culinary herbs. Frozen herbs don't have such a long storage life as air-dried plants, but they can be kept for about six months. Parsley, savory, mint, marjoram, sorrel, chives and fennel all freeze well. Once herbs have been frozen, they tend to lose their texture, so you can't use them as a garnish. For long-term storage, blanch the herbs by dipping them first in boiling water and then in cold water, before placing them in freezer bags.

Freezing herbs in ice cubes

Herbs can also be frozen as ice cubes.

Single mint leaves, borage flowers and marigold petals all freeze well in ice cubes, as do chopped parsley and chives.

STAGE 1: Chop the leaves and place them in ice trays. Fill the trays with water and freeze.

STAGE 2: Store in plastic bags when frozen.

PRESERVING IN OIL AND VINEGAR

In medieval times, herbs and flowers were preserved in oil or vinegar and this method is still used today.

Flowers

Use a good white wine vinegar for flowers such as lavender, mint, basil, thyme and rosemary, and a cider vinegar for darker flowers such as sweet violets and red roses. Remove all stalks, green parts and white heels of the petals before using and steep the scented flowers in the vinegar, or oil, for three to four weeks. Leave the bottles to stand on a sunny windowsill, turning them at regular intervals to allow the sun to release the flowers' natural oils. Give them a good shake each day.

Scented flowers go well with oils such as sunflower or safflower, while aromatic herb flowers complement a richer oil: hazelnut or olive, for example. It is best to use your flower oils within three months; although they will last longer – up to six months – if the flowers are removed. Try lavender, jasmine and rose petals in a light oil, and flowering herbs such as mint, marjoram, thyme, dill and fennel in an olive or hazelnut oil.

Leaves

The leaves of tarragon, basil, dill, fennel, mint, summer savory and salad burnet make

Basil can be preserved in good-quality olive oil

Herb oils should be stored away from sunlight

Bottles of herb oils and vinegars

CANDYING HERB FLOWERS

Some herb flowers can be candied to preserve them. Try violets, lavender, rosemary, sage, mint and bergamot. Lemon balm leaves can also be candied. Remember to check that the flowers you use are edible, as many of them are not.

You will need:
Violets, gathered on a sunny morning
    after the dew has dried
1 egg white
Caster sugar
Whisk
Tweezers (optional)
Wire rack or baking tray
Greaseproof paper

excellent vinegars. Wash and dry the leaves, pack them into a wide-necked jar and pour in the vinegar. White wine vinegar is best for basil, tarragon and salad burnet and cider vinegar for mint. Screw the lid on tightly and stand the jar on the windowsill for ten days, shaking it every day. If, after ten days, the taste isn't strong enough, take out the leaves, strain the vinegar and add new leaves. Repeat the process until you are satisfied with the strength of the flavour, then strain the vinegar into bottles and add a sprig of the herb before sealing. Label and date.

Herb oils can be made from the leaves of basil, tarragon, thyme, fennel and rosemary. Crush the leaves, place in a wide-necked jar and pour over the oil. Leave the jar in the sunlight for two to three weeks, shaking every day. Then, strain off the leaves and repeat the process until you have the strength of flavour you require. Strain the oil into bottles, add a sprig of the herb, and seal tightly. Label and date.

STAGE 1: Whisk the egg white in a bowl until frothy.

STAGE 2: Dip the violets in the egg white, one by one, so that each bloom is well coated. Use tweezers to hold them if you wish. Shake off any surplus egg white.

STAGE 3: Dip the damp violets individually in the caster sugar.

STAGE 4: Place on a wire rack or baking tray lined with greasproof paper, positioning them so that they do not touch each other.

STAGE 5: Place in an open oven with the temperature on the lowest setting, and dry slowly.

STAGE 6: When they are completely dry and brittle, remove from the oven and store between sheets of greaseproof paper in an airtight container.

HERB FLOWER SUGARS

Herb flowers can be made into flower sugars by pounding the flowers with three times their own weight of caster sugar and storing in glass jars away from direct light. Suitable flowers for this method are violets, lavender, jasmine, rosemary and rose petals.

CANDIED ANGELICA

Pencil-thin stems of angelica harvested in early summer can be preserved in sugar. Cut the stems into 7.5–10cm (3–4in) lengths, boil in a little water until tender, drain and peel off the outer skin. Simmer again until bright green. Dry the stems on kitchen paper and weigh them. Place in a shallow dish, and add an equal weight of sugar, sprinkled over the stems. Leave for two days. Boil the mixture, making more syrup if necessary, for ten minutes. Drain, then spread the stems on a rack to dry thoroughly.

More ideas for preserving

- Herbs can be preserved in salt, an old-fashioned method of storage where layers of herbs – the leaves of basil, for example – are alternated with layers of coarse salt in a wide-necked jar. Olive oil is then poured over and the jar tightly sealed. It can be kept in the refrigerator for several weeks.
- Keep dried bay leaves on a long stalk and store in a tall, glass jar in a dark corner of the kitchen.
- Herb leaves and flowers can be preserved by pressing in flower presses. Use them to make pictures, greetings cards and book marks.
- Place dried parsley, thyme and a bay leaf in muslin as a bouquet garni. Store in an airtight jar and use for marinades and in stews, casseroles and soups.
- Soak nasturtium seeds overnight in salt water. Then pickle in vinegar, and eat them as you would capers.

Store candied angelica in an airtight jar

Bouquet garni of fresh herbs, and dried in muslin

GLOSSARY OF GARDENING TERMS

ACID A term applied to soil with a pH content of less than 7.0. The soil is deficient in lime and contains few basic minerals.

ALKALINE Usually indicates a soil derived from chalk or limestone with a pH reading of more than 7.0. Most herbs will thrive in alkaline soil.

ANNUAL A plant that is grown from seed and that germinates, flowers, seeds and dies all within one growing season.

BIENNIAL A plant which completes its life cycle in two years. It produces stems and leaves during the first year and flowers in the second, after which it sets seed and dies.

BRACT A small modified leaf, often protective, at the base of a flower.

Caraway is a biennial herb that dies back in its first winter

BROADCAST The scattering of seed evenly over an area of ground rather than sowing in drills.

BULB An underground stem consisting of fleshy scales that store food for the embryo plant.

CEMENT A mixture of sand, cement and water.

CLOCHE A portable, tunnel-shaped structure made of glass or clear plastic, and used to protect the early growth of crops in open ground.

COLD FRAME A glazed structure, usually made from bricks, with a movable cover of glass or clear plastic. Unheated, it is used to protect plants during winter.

COMPOST

1 A growing medium comprising mainly of peat, loam, sand, leaf mould, or other ingredients, in which seeds are sown and plants are potted.

2 Recycled, decomposed plant material and other organic matter used as a soil improver and as a mulch.

CONCRETE A mixture of cement, sand, gravel and water.

CROCKS Broken pieces of clay pots, placed in the bottom of a container to provide drainage and air circulation to the root system of the plants.

CROWN The basal part of a herbaceous perennial, situated at or just below the surface of the soil from which the roots and shoots grow.

CULTIVAR A variety of plant that has been cultivated, rather than one that grows naturally in the wild.

CUTTING A piece of stem, root, shoot, bud or leaf that is cut off the parent plant to be used as a method for increasing numbers of that plant.

DEAD HEAD To remove spent flower or flowerheads, usually to encourage further growth or more flowering and to prevent self-seeding.

DECIDUOUS Plants, especially trees and shrubs, that lose their leaves at the end of the growing season. These are then renewed at the start of the next growing season.

DIVISION A method of increasing plants by which the roots are divided into two or more parts during dormancy.

DORMANCY Term applied to the resting period of a seed or plant when there is a temporary slowing or cessation of growth. Usually occurs in winter.

DOUBLE DIGGING When the soil is dug to two spades' depth.

DRILL A straight furrow made in the soil for sowing seed in a line.

EVERGREEN Plants, mostly shrubs and trees, that keep most of their leaves all year round, although some of the older leaves are regularly lost throughout the year. They provide structure in the garden during the winter.

FIBROUS Thin, fibre-like mass of roots, often branching and dense.

GERMINATION The changes that take place as a seed starts to grow and the root and shoot emerge.

GROUND COVER Low-growing plants that cover the ground quickly and suppress the growth of weeds.

HABIT The characteristic shape and general appearance of a plant.

Hyssop is a perennial evergreen shrub

HALF-HARDY Half-hardy plants may not survive severe frosts, but the term generally applies to plants that will successfully over-winter outdoors in a sheltered position.

HARDENED OFF The technique for acclimatizing young plants to outside temperatures. Plants should be placed outside during the day for increasing lengths of time and then put back under cover at night. This process can take two or three weeks.

HARDY Plants able to survive the winter outdoors, including frosty conditions, without protection.

HARDCORE Pieces of broken terracotta pots or gravel placed in the bottom of containers to help drainage. Also gravel packed under paving or concrete to give it a firm base.

HERBACEOUS Usually refers to plants with non-woody stems that die down at the end of each growing season.

Tansy has a strong, invasive root system

HUMUS Crumbly, dark brown, decayed vegetable matter brought about by the partial breakdown of plant remains by bacteria. An example is well-made garden compost.

HYBRID A plant created from parents of different species or genera.

INFUSION A liquid obtained by steeping herbs in boiling water.

INVASIVE A vigorous-growing plant that will suffocate neighbouring plants if not contained or controlled.

LANCEOLATE A narrow, spear-head-like shape , tapering at both ends. Applies to leaf shape.

LAYERING A method of propagation whereby a stem is pegged down into the soil and induced to root while still attached to the parent plant.

LIME Compounds of calcium. Some soils have a predominant lime content. The amount of lime determines whether a soil is acid, neutral or alkaline.

LOAM Soil made up of an even mixture of clay and sand, with a balanced mixture of nutrients. It is well-drained, fertile and moisture retentive.

MULCH A layer of material applied to the soil surface to conserve moisture, protect plant roots from frost, improve soil structure and suppress weeds.

NODE The point on a stem from which leaves, shoots, branches or flowers arise.

NUTRIENTS Minerals used to develop proteins and other compounds necessary to the growth and well-being of a plant.

OVATE Egg shaped, broader at the base, and more pointed at the tip. Applies to leaves.

PEAT Partly decayed organic matter, usually acid, with an excellent water-retaining structure. Used in growing composts or mulches, although peat substitutes, such as coconut fibre, are now often used for environmental reasons.

PERENNIAL Any plant that lives for at least three seasons. It flowers every year, dying down in winter, with new shoots appearing each spring. Usually the term applied to herbaceous plants. Woody-based perennials only die down partially.

pH A scale of measurement that indicates the acidity or alkalinity of soil. The scale ranges from 1–14; pH 7 is neutral, below 7 is acid, above is alkaline.

Feverfew is a decorative, hardy perennial

PINCHING OUT The removal of the growing tips of a plant, using the finger and thumb, to encourage the production of side-shoots. Also known as 'stopping'.

PRICK OUT Transfer of seedlings from the container or bed in which they germinated to alternative pots or soil where they have room to develop and grow.

PROPAGATION Increasing plants vegetatively or by seed.

PROSTRATE Growing low or flat over the surface of the ground.

RUNNER A slender, horizontally spreading stem that runs along the surface of the soil, rooting at intervals.

SELF-SEED Plants that shed their seeds around them after flowering, from which new plants will grow the following year.

SPECIES A classification applying to plants of the same specific kind. Individual plants that breed together and have the same constant characters. Species grown from seed are consistently true to type.

TAP ROOT The main root of a plant that grows downwards. Long and strong, it stretches down into the soil.

Variegated lemon thyme has multi-coloured leaves

TENDER Term applied to plants that are susceptible to damage at low temperatures. They cannot survive outside during winter and should be brought indoors as they are vulnerable to frost damage.

TILTH Soil broken down into small crumbs by correct digging and raking. An ideal, fine, crumbly, top layer of soil.

TOPIARY The art of clipping and training dense-leaved shrubs and trees into geometric and unusual shapes.

TOPSOIL The fertile, uppermost layer of soil in which most plants root.

Umbel A flat-topped or rounded flower cluster on individual flower stalks radiating from one central point.

VARIEGATED A word used to describe leaves (or flowers) that exhibit more than one colour. Generally used to describe leaves with white or cream markings.

VARIETY A word used to describe a variant from an original species or hybrid. Now often used to describe variants induced by cultivation (cultivars).

WHORL Three or more leaves or flowers forming a ring at one stem joint.

Angelica is a biennial that sets seed in its second year, and which is best propagated from seed

ABOUT THE AUTHOR

Yvonne Cuthbertson discovered the joys of herb gardening some years ago when she and her family moved into a non-working farm. It came complete with two acres of uncultivated farmland where she set about making a large herb garden. This was just the start of her fascination with herbs and, as the years progressed, more house moves have enabled her to make several more such gardens.

A former primary-school head teacher, Yvonne holds a Royal Horticultural Society General Certificate in Horticulture. She has written for a variety of publications, both in Britain and abroad, on topics including gardening, herbalism, antiques, conservation and alternative medicine. She often combines her love of writing with a passion for photography.

Yvonne and her husband have recently moved to Northern Ireland, while their daughter is a student at University College, London.

INDEX

Page numbers in **bold** include illustrations of herb. Page numbers in *italics* indicate main references to herbs

GMC Publications

BOOKS

WOODWORKING

Advanced Scrollsaw Projects	GMC Publications
Beginning Picture Marquetry	Lawrence Threadgold
Bird Boxes and Feeders for the Garden	Dave Mackenzie
Celtic Carved Lovespoons: 30 Patterns	Sharon Littley & Clive Griffin
Celtic Woodcraft	Glenda Bennett
Complete Woodfinishing (Revised Edition)	Ian Hosker
David Charlesworth's Furniture-Making Techniques	David Charlesworth
David Charlesworth's Furniture-Making Techniques – Volume 2	David Charlesworth
The Encyclopedia of Joint Making	Terrie Noll
Furniture-Making Projects for the Wood Craftsman	GMC Publications
Furniture-Making Techniques for the Wood Craftsman	GMC Publications
Furniture Projects with the Router	Kevin Ley
Furniture Restoration (Practical Crafts)	Kevin Jan Bonner
Furniture Restoration: A Professional at Work	John Lloyd
Furniture Restoration and Repair for Beginners	Kevin Jan Bonner
Furniture Restoration Workshop	Kevin Jan Bonner
Green Woodwork	Mike Abbott
Intarsia: 30 Patterns for the Scrollsaw	John Everett
Kevin Ley's Furniture Projects	Kevin Ley
Making Chairs and Tables	GMC Publications
Making Chairs and Tables – Volume 2	GMC Publications
Making Classic English Furniture	Paul Richardson
Making Heirloom Boxes	Peter Lloyd
Making Screw Threads in Wood	Fred Holder
Making Shaker Furniture	Barry Jackson
Making Woodwork Aids and Devices	Robert Wearing
Mastering the Router	Ron Fox
Pine Furniture Projects for the Home	Dave Mackenzie
Practical Scrollsaw Patterns	John Everett
Router Magic: Jigs, Fixtures and Tricks to Unleash your Router's Full Potential	Bill Hylton
Router Tips & Techniques	Robert Wearing
Routing: A Workshop Handbook	Anthony Bailey
Routing for Beginners	Anthony Bailey
Sharpening: The Complete Guide	Jim Kingshott
Sharpening Pocket Reference Book	Jim Kingshott
Simple Scrollsaw Projects	GMC Publications
Space-Saving Furniture Projects	Dave Mackenzie
Stickmaking: A Complete Course	Andrew Jones & Clive George
Stickmaking Handbook	Andrew Jones & Clive George
Storage Projects for the Router	GMC Publications
Test Reports: The Router and Furniture & Cabinetmaking	GMC Publications
Veneering: A Complete Course	Ian Hosker
Veneering Handbook	Ian Hosker
Woodfinishing Handbook (Practical Crafts)	Ian Hosker
Woodworking with the Router: Professional Router Techniques any Woodworker can Use	Bill Hylton & Fred Matlack

DOLLS' HOUSES AND MINIATURES

1/12 Scale Character Figures for the Dolls' House	James Carrington
Americana in 1/12 Scale: 50 Authentic Projects	Joanne Ogreenc & Mary Lou Santovec
Architecture for Dolls' Houses	Joyce Percival
The Authentic Georgian Dolls' House	Brian Long
A Beginners' Guide to the Dolls' House Hobby	Jean Nisbett
Celtic, Medieval and Tudor Wall Hangings in 1/12 Scale Needlepoint	Sandra Whitehead
Creating Decorative Fabrics: Projects in 1/12 Scale	Janet Storey
The Dolls' House 1/24 Scale: A Complete Introduction	Jean Nisbett
Dolls' House Accessories, Fixtures and Fittings	Andrea Barham
Dolls' House Furniture: Easy-to-Make Projects in 1/12 Scale	Freida Gray
Dolls' House Makeovers	Jean Nisbett
Dolls' House Window Treatments	Eve Harwood
Easy to Make Dolls' House Accessories	Andrea Barham
Edwardian-Style Hand-Knitted Fashion for 1/12 Scale Dolls	Yvonne Wakefield
How to Make Your Dolls' House Special: Fresh Ideas for Decorating	Beryl Armstrong
Make Your Own Dolls' House Furniture	Maurice Harper
Making Dolls' House Furniture	Patricia King
Making Georgian Dolls' Houses	Derek Rowbottom
Making Miniature Chinese Rugs and Carpets	Carol Phillipson
Making Miniature Food and Market Stalls	Angie Scarr
Making Miniature Gardens	Freida Gray
Making Miniature Oriental Rugs & Carpets	Meik & Ian McNaughton
Making Period Dolls' House Accessories	Andrea Barham
Making Tudor Dolls' Houses	Derek Rowbottom
Making Victorian Dolls' House Furniture	Patricia King
Medieval and Tudor Needlecraft: Knights and Ladies in 1/12 Scale	Sandra Whitehead
Miniature Bobbin Lace	Roz Snowden
Miniature Embroidery for the Georgian Dolls' House	Pamela Warner
Miniature Embroidery for the Tudor and Stuart Dolls' House	Pamela Warner
Miniature Embroidery for the Victorian Dolls' House	Pamela Warner
Miniature Needlepoint Carpets	Janet Granger
More Miniature Oriental Rugs & Carpets	Meik & Ian McNaughton
Needlepoint 1/12 Scale: Design Collections for the Dolls' House	Felicity Price
New Ideas for Miniature Bobbin Lace	Roz Snowden
Patchwork Quilts for the Dolls' House: 20 Projects in 1/12 Scale	Sarah Williams

CRAFTS

American Patchwork Designs in Needlepoint	Melanie Tacon
Bargello: A Fresh Approach to Florentine Embroidery	Brenda Day
Beginning Picture Marquetry	Lawrence Threadgold
Blackwork: A New Approach	Brenda Day
Celtic Cross Stitch Designs	Carol Phillipson
Celtic Knotwork Designs	Sheila Sturrock
Celtic Knotwork Handbook	Sheila Sturrock
Celtic Spirals and Other Designs	Sheila Sturrock
Complete Pyrography	Stephen Poole
Creating Made-to-Measure Knitwear: A Revolutionary Approach to Knitwear Design	Sylvia Wynn

MAGAZINES
WOODTURNING ◆ WOODCARVING ◆ FURNITURE & CABINETMAKING ◆ THE ROUTER
NEW WOODWORKING ◆ THE DOLLS' HOUSE MAGAZINE ◆ OUTDOOR PHOTOGRAPHY
BLACK & WHITE PHOTOGRAPHY ◆ TRAVEL PHOTOGRAPHY
MACHINE KNITTING NEWS ◆ BUSINESSMATTERS

The above represents a selection of titles currently published or scheduled to be published.
All are available direct from the Publishers or through bookshops, newsagents and specialist retailers.

To place an order, or to obtain a complete catalogue, contact:

GMC Publications, 166 High Street, Lewes, East Sussex BN7 1XU, United Kingdom
Tel: 01273 488005 Fax: 01273 478606 ◆ E-mail: pubs@thegmcgroup.com

Orders by credit card are accepted